1970

TH'UPRIGHT HEART
AND PURE

DUQUESNE STUDIES
PHILOLOGICAL SERIES
10

TH'UPRIGHT
HEART AND PURE

Essays on John Milton Commemorating
the Tercentenary of the Publication
of Paradise Lost

edited by AMADEUS P. FIORE, O.F.M.

SIENA COLLEGE

DUQUESNE UNIVERSITY PRESS
Pittsburgh, Pa.
Editions E. Nauwelaerts, Louvain

DUQUESNE STUDIES

PHILOLOGICAL SERIES

Volume One—Calvin Huckabay, *John Milton: A Bibliographical Supplement 1929–1957*. xi and 211 pages. Price: $6.25.

Volume Two—Joseph A. Lauritis, C.S.Sp., Vernon F. Gallagher, C.S.Sp., Ralph A. Klinefelter, *A Critical Edition of John Lydgate's Life of Our Lady*. ix and 742 pages. Price: $12.50.

Volume Three—Waldo F. McNeir and Foster Provost, *Annotated Bibliography of Edmund Spenser, 1937–1960*. Out of print.

Volume Four—Dorothy Clotelle Clarke, *Morphology of Fifteenth Century Castilian Verse*. vii and 233 pages. Price: $6.95. An M.H.R.A. Monograph.

Volume Five—Herbert H. Petit, general editor, *Essays and Studies in Language and Literature*. vi and 218 pages. Price: $6.25.

Volume Six—Arthur Hill Cash, *Sterne's Comedy of Moral Sentiments: The Ethical Dimension of the Journey*. 152 pages. Price: $4.25. An M.H.R.A. Monograph.

Volume Seven—John R. Roberts, *A Critical Anthology of English Recusant Devotional Prose, 1558–1603*. 322 pages. Price: $6.95.

Volume Eight—Velma Bourgeois Richmond, *Laments for the Dead in Medieval Narrative*. 199 pages. Price: $7.95.

Volume Nine—Ione Kemp Knight, *Wimbledon's Sermon*. 155 pages. $7.95.

Library of Congress Catalog Card Number 67–28898

For my Mother *and* Father

CONTENTS

PREFACE   5
  Amadeus P. Fiore, O.F.M.

MILTON'S LIMBO OF VANITY
  Merritt Y. Hughes   7

THE HERESIES OF SATAN
  William B. Hunter, Jr.   25

THE COMPOSITION OF MILTON'S
DE DOCTRINA CHRISTIANA: FIRST PHASE
  Maurice Kelley   35

MILTON AS SATIRIST AND WIT
  Edward Le Comte   45

JERUSALEM AND ATHENS: THE TEMPTATION
OF LEARNING IN PARADISE REGAINED
  B. Rajan   61

THE METAPHOR OF INSPIRATION IN
PARADISE LOST
  John T. Shawcross   75

Contents

PARADISE LOST AND THE ITALIAN
EPIC TRADITION
Wayne Shumaker   87

THE TRAGIC GLASS: MILTON, MINTURNO
AND THE CONDITION HUMAINE
John M. Steadman   101

MILTON AND THE HUNDRED ARTICLES
AGAINST ALEXANDER MORE
Kester Svendsen   117

MILTON AS PHILOSOPHICAL POET
Robert West   131

A NOTE ON MILTON'S DICTION
B. A. Wright   143

PREFACE

The contributors to this volume, upon invitation of the editor, have graciously submitted these original essays on Milton in commemoration of the tercentenary of the publication of *Paradise Lost*. It is of no little significance that a Milton tercentenary should occur during an age of ideological ferment, especially since Milton's life and works reflect an age of theological and political upheaval not too unlike our own. And like that of many twentieth-century thinkers, his life vocation was that of poet-priest-prophet; his life concern was to see England and the world a celestial city; and his preoccupation as a layman was the revitalization of the English church as well as of the English government.

I regret that it was impossible for various reasons to include many more fine scholar-critics in this collection, but Milton critics have flourished in our time, and a single volume cannot do justice to them all. The principle of eminence and excellence of particular scholars in the world of Milton criticism was the prime basis for my choice of contributors. All eleven are universal scholars in the international community of learned men. All American contributors are members of the Milton Society of America. All in one way or another have been instrumental in restoring Milton to his true stature after a brief and somewhat insignificant dislodgment during the early part of this century. And all of them are known for their exemplary scholarship, their verve and their sensitivity of critical perception, and above all, like Milton, their humanism.

Originally these essays were to be published in Greyfriar, the literary journal printed at Siena College. But the expense, the restriction of space, and the limitation of circulation made this undesirable, if not impossible. The Duquesne University Press kindly offered to publish the essays in book form. To my contributors and to my publisher, I am very much indebted.

AMADEUS P. FIORE, O.F.M.
Siena College

MILTON'S LIMBO
OF VANITY

Merritt Y. Hughes

Milton's allegory of things to come interrupts Satan's epic flight
from Hell across Chaos to find Adam and Eve in Eden. He has
landed on the storm-swept hull of the newly created universe.

So on this windie Sea of Land, the Fiend	440
Walk'd up and down alone bent on his prey,	
Alone, for other Creature in this place	
Living or liveless to be found was none,	
None yet, but store hereafter from the earth	
Up hither like Aereal vapours flew	445
Of all things transitorie and vain, when Sin	
With vanity had filld the works of men:	
Both all things vain, and all who in vain things	
Built thir fond hopes of Glorie or lasting fame,	
Or happiness in this or th' other life;	450
All who have thir reward on Earth, the fruits	
Of painful Superstition and blind Zeal,	
Naught seeking but the praise of men, here find	
Fit retribution, emptie as their deeds;	
All th' unaccomplisht works of Natures hand,	455
Abortive, monstrous, or unkindly mixt,	

Dissolvd on Earth, fleet hither, and in vain,
Till final dissolution, wander here,
Not in the neighbouring Moon, as some have dreamd;
Those   argent   Fields   more   likely   habitants,   460
Translated Saints, or middle Spirits hold
Betwixt th' Angelical and Human kinde:
Hither of ill-joynd Sons and Daughters born
First from the ancient World those Giants came
With many a vain exploit, though then renownd: 465
The builders next of *Babel* on the Plain
Of *Sennaar,* and still with vain designe
New *Babels,* had they wherewithall, would build:
Others came single; he who to be deemd
A God, leap'd fondly into *AEtna* flames,   470
Empedocles, and hee who to enjoy
Plato's Elysium, leap'd into the Sea,
Cleombrotus, and many more too long,
Embryo's and Idiots, Eremits and Friers
White, Black and Grey, with all their trumperie.   475
Here Pilgrims roam, that stray'd so farr to seek
In *Golgotha* him dead, who lives in Heav'n;
And they who to be sure of Paradise
Dying put on the weeds of *Dominic,*
Or in *Franciscan* think to pass disguis'd;   480
They pass the Planets seven, and pass the fixt,
And that Crystalline Sphear whose ballance weighs
The Trepidation talkt, and that first mov'd;
And now Saint *Peter* at Heav'ns Wicket seems
To wait them with his Keys, and now at foot   485
Of Heav'ns ascent they lift their Feet, when loe
A violent cross wind from either Coast
Blows them transverse ten thousand Leagues awry
Into the devious Air; then might ye see
Cowles, Hoods and Habits with thir wearers tost   490
And flutterd into Raggs, then Reliques, Beads,

Indulgences, Dispenses, Pardons, Bulls,
The sport of Winds: all these upwhirld aloft
Fly o're the backside of the World farr off
Into a *Limbo* large and broad, since calld   495
The Paradise of Fools, to few unknown
Long after, now unpeopl'd and untrod; . . .

Fascinated and perhaps disgusted by Milton's Limbo, many readers suffer it impatiently as an outcropping of religious bigotry blocking the channel of the epic narrative in *Paradise Lost*. It has been deplored since Addison condemned its disregard of Aristotle's principle of narrative integrity and its indulgence in satirical allegory unbecoming an epic poem.[1] Addison and Dr. Johnson both bracketed the passage with the allegorical episode of Sin as the motherless daughter of Satan and incestuous mother of Death,[2] which Johnson called[3] "one of the greatest faults in the poem." From such criticism Milton's best way of escape may seem to be by way of Richard Bentley's assumption[4] that the Paradise of Fools was one of many interpolations easily detected by their "silliness and unfitness," which were injected by an editor who presumably took advantage of Milton's blindness to tamper with the first edition of the poem.

I

But the Limbo of Fools is patently Miltonic. Links with the prose works only less distinct than those noted below are more than sufficient to establish the authorship. In a candid study entitled "Milton, Limbo, and Suicide,"[5] Joseph Horrell sees Milton's hand at work in every line of the passage while he treats it as esthetically no more valid than it seemed to the eighteenth century critics. His essay is important for its revelation of the background of Milton's suicides, Empedocles and Cleombrotus; but his main interest is in his critical distinction of the passage as an "improbable picture" rather than as an " 'improbable action' according to Aristotle's terms." For many readers he may enhance the psychological interest of the passage by treating it as a wilfully personal "interpolation [of which Milton] must have thought highly, with a strong urge to use it, or he would hardly have let it play havoc with his context," or have "subverted his cosmology to satire" for its sake.

Though the subversion of Milton's allegory to his satire has been defended by Frank L. Huntley in "A Justification of Milton's Paradise of Fools,"[6] there has been little discussion of his vindication of it on the basis of its thematic links with the last two books of the epic. Nor has any editor yet taken account of Miss Moritz-Siebeck's even more elaborate contextual analysis of the passage.[7] Dislike of it simply as allegory is largely a matter of prejudice which is becoming less and less sure of itself as a general principle. As allegory, one of the most interesting things about it is its final integration into the narrative action by means of the very different, traditional allegory of the ladder of light which Jacob saw in his vision in the field at Luz,[8] linking Heaven and Earth and crowded with "angels ascending and descending upon it." The allegory of Limbo gives way to the more familiar one which theologians had allegorized as an eternal stair with Angels descending on it to minister to men, or as a symbol of Christ on the cross, or (in the words of the Cambridge Platonist, Peter Sterry) as typifying the "mystical steps" in the scale of universal nature, descending "from its purest heighth, by beautiful, harmonious, just degrees and steps . . . into every Being."[9] The light surrounding these "mysteriously meant" stairs shows Satan his way into the newly created universe, and with his entry the main epic narrative is resumed.

Unlike the allegory of Jacob's dream, Milton's allegorical Limbo has some conspicuous elements of historical fact mixed in it, and some of these link it thematically with the visions of yet unenacted human history which are to figure prominently in Michael's dialogue with Adam in Books XI and XII. The method is described by Huntley as a kind of reversal of the cinema flashback. Readers are carried "forward imaginatively [to] a future crowd journeying *backward* from Earth up to this wind-swept plain" on the outside of the universe from which Satan has just found his way inside. The crowd's leaders are the " 'False-titl'd Sons of God [who] roaming the Earth / Cast wanton eyes on the daughters of men"[10] and so plunged humanity into an endless pursuit of false glory." Their appearance here together with the builders of the Tower of Babel prepares for the appearance of the giant sons of those miscegenated marriages in Book XI, 688–697, and of the builders of Babel in XII, 38–47. So there is a double link between the Paradise of Fools and the historical consequences of the Fall as Michael represents them to Adam in the last books of the poem.

To many readers Milton's condemnation of the Giants in Book XI and of the builders of Babel in Book XII may seem too severe for him ever to have thought of them as belonging in his Limbo. An answer to the objection has been unintentionally provided by Professor E. L. Marilla[11] in his incidental remark in a study of "Milton's Paradise of Fools" that, "The builders of Babel were not violators of conscience; they were simply victims of the same overweening pride that has inspired many a subsequent Utopian dreamer." This seems to tally with Milton's statement of the object of the builders as

> To get themselves a name, least far disperst
> In foraign Lands thir memorie be lost
> Regardless whether good or evil fame.　　(XII, 45–47)

The sin of the builders hardly seems deserving of a worse final punishment than that of the "final dissolution" which Milton assigns to all the denizens of his Limbo. Because the "Builders of *Babel* on the plain / Of *Sennaar*" are always being reborn in the world,

> 　and still with vain designe
> New *Babels,* had they wherewithall, would build,
> 　　　　　　　　　　　　(III, 466–468)

they do seem to belong in Milton's Paradise of Fools, but it is a
rash conclusion to put their master there. Can Milton be suggesting an end like that of his followers for Nimrod, the tyrant of
God in Genesis 10. 8–10 and 11. 2–9, the man who is destined
to

> arrogate Dominion undeserv'd
> Over his brethren, and quite dispossess
> Concord and law of Nature from the Earth;
>
> (XII. 27–29)

Professor Marilla's interest in Milton's Limbo is concerned
with its resemblances to Plato's treatment of the transmigrating
souls in the vision of Er in the *Republic*. Most of the souls are on
their way to reincarnation. The few who are seemingly endlessly
detained in Hades have lived the most evil lives. Their leader is
the archetypal tyrant Ardiaeus. Er reports seeing him subjected
to the most contumelious and violent torture. Milton never indul-
ges in fancies about the punishment of individual sinners in any
hell, but he probably saw no injustice in Dante's portrayal of
Nimrod in the twelfth canto of the *Purgatory*. There, for the
edification of the souls in need of purgation from the sin of pride,
Dante saw Nimrod, the subverter of the civic virtue of multitudes, represented in worn bas-relief in a composite portrayal of
the proudest figures in history and scripture, with Satan standing
first:

> At foot of the stupendous work he stood,
> As if bewildered, looking on the crowd
> Leagued in his proud attempt on Sennaar's plain.
>
> (Cary's translation)

II

Milton's biblical figures are still easily recognizable, as one at
least of his classical figures in Limbo may not be. Its scope is
universal and its two biblical examples are balanced with two
classical philosophers, the first of whom, Empedocles, was, like

Nimrod, almost too powerful a character to belong in the company of Milton's fools. Readers of Horace would remember the reference in the *Ars poetica* (464–466) to Empedocles, the philosopher-poet who, because he hoped to be remembered as having been immortally exalted into the company of the gods, made the coolly calculated decision to leap into the burning crater of Mt. Aetna:

> Deus inmortalis haberi
> Dum cupit Empedocles, ardentem frigidus Aetnam
> Insiluit.

Readers of Dante would have a very different image of him standing gravely among the philosophers and poets of antiquity in the quiet region just inside Hell's gates (*Inferno,* IV. 138). The more familiar Horatian context puts him into the shabby society of mad poets who stumble into pits and deserve no rescue from their folly. Though the surviving fragments of Empedocles' poem περὶ φύσεως (On Nature) may justify his honorable company in the *Inferno,* his character is not taken seriously in Diogenes Laertius' account of his life. Milton's interest in that biographical essay can be assumed, for he put the *Lives of the Eminent Philosophers* on his reading list for the last year of his ideal school in *Of Education.*[12] Laertes is objective in recording Empedocles' reputation in Sicily as a medical and meteorological wonder-worker. Readers are left free to choose among several conflicting accounts of his death. One was a servant's report that he had been translated to heaven at midnight when a bright light suddenly irradiated the house, and a mysterious voice was heard calling his master away. Other accounts represented him as dying a natural death in Agrigentum or in exile in the Pelopennesus. In a closing epigram on the doubtfully attested assumption into heaven from Mt. Aetna, Laertes treated what may have happened as a probably fatal accident in an unfortunate attempt to abscond, leaving the impression that the vanished man had been caught up into the company of the gods. Regarding Empedocles' death as an attempt to achieve deification—either in reality or in popular acclaim—Milton could consider it a ridiculous indulgence of the vain human hope "of Glory or lasting fame." He could hardly think of it as something like the climax of a modern "dialogue of the mind with itself," such as Arnold was to make it in *Empedocles on Aetna*. To a Christian meditating either Horace's lines or Laertius' epigram on Empedocles, his end might seem like a pagan travesty of the assumption of the prophet Elijah to heaven "in a whirlwind," and seemingly "in a chariot of fire."[13]

Contempt for Empedocles' death as a foolishly motivated suicide figured in some of the Christian apologies of the Fathers of the Church. Horrell shows that it was one of many examples of the evil effects of the false wisdom of the pagan philosophers which Lactantius adduced in the third book of his *Divine Institutes*. And in Milton's link of Empedocles with Cleombrotus, Horrell also spots a reason for suspecting that Lactantius was in his mind. Lactantius simply mentions the two men in a list of philosophers whose lives were for various reasons understood to have ended in variously motivated suicides. Two of them were the Stoic founders Cleanthes and Zeno. In Milton's eyes Cleombrotus can hardly have been tainted with Stoicism, that nurse of philosophic pride which he condemned in *Paradise Regained* (IV. 300). The little that is known of Cleombrotus suggests neither the kind of pride for which the Stoics were blamed, nor that of the thaumaturge Empedocles. It rather suggests the self-absorption of an idealistic youth for whom suicide had become the test of his dedication to the philosophic life. The linked figures are contrasted. Cleombrotus is a means of transition from inveterate lust of glory in old age to youth's willingness to die obscurely as a way to join the company of the great and wise dead.

Cleombrotus was a student of Plato who happened, it seems, to be in Aegina at the time of Socrates' death. His suicide was not a response to that event. Traditionally, it was understood to have been impelled by a too ardent faith in the immortality which Socrates is quoted in the *Phaedo* as attributing to all wise men. Some of his friends, as they listened to his reasoning in that last afternoon of his life, misunderstood him to be recommending suicide as the right and sure way to enjoyment of the life which all true philosophers have sought. Later, when Cleombrotus read the *Phaedo,* he also misunderstood Socrates and sought admission to the immortal company of the wise by plunging to his death. A century later, when his act and motive had become an ambivalent tradition, Callimachus wrote an epigram about them. As an official in the library of Ptolemy Philadelphus in Alexandria, Callimachus was in a position somewhat like that of a modern college dean. There seems to have been a wave of suicides among the students of an indiscreetly emotional lecturer on the *Phaedo* whose classes were finally closed for the public good by Ptolemy. Callimachus' epigram has been read as an attack on Plato's work, but it may also be taken as the appeal of a responsible educator for pity, but at the same time for an end to fanatical admiration of the young man who had plunged to his death long ago, not because he had suffered any harm which only death could cure, but simply because he had read one work of Plato on the soul:

Εἶπας ""Ἤλιε Χαῖρε" Κλεόμβροτος Ὠμβρακιώτης ἧλατ’ ἀφ’ ὑψηλοῦ τείχεος εἰς Ἀίδην ἄξιον οὐδὲν ἰδὼν θανάτου κακόν, αλλα Πλάτωνος ἐν τὸ περὶ ψυχῆς γράμμ’ ἀναλεξάμενος.[14]

The epigram does not really shed much light upon the motives for Cleombrotus' suicide. To a Christian apologist like Lactantius it was simply the evil fruit of the teaching of the noblest of the pagan philosophers. Milton's contemporaries were almost as severe in their judgment of "that heathen Cleombrotus," as Bishop Joseph Hall called him for acting upon pagan teaching about immortality "in a blinde love to his soule and out of bare opinion."[15] In a carefully pondered paragraph in *The Monarchie of Man* the first distinguished leader of resistance to King Charles to die in prison, Sir John Eliot, asked: "Why doe we not . . . , as

Cleombrotus, haveing re'dd *Platoes* discourses on the immortali-
tie of the Soule, precipitate our selves, hasten to that excellence,
presse to that rich magazine of treasures?"[16] Eliot answered the
question in Plato's terms: death should come only at the will of
the gods. In this Milton would have concurred. But if he had
been asked why Cleombrotus was given the dubious honor of
mention by name in his Limbo, he would have replied in terms
rather like those of Bishop Hall. Instead of "bare opinion," however, he would have used the term "implicit faith"—the surrender of the right and duty of individual judgment about the great
issues of life to any authority except a man's own carefully
exercised intelligence. His final word on that point was delivered
in *Of True Religion, Heresie, Schism,* when he declared "implicit
faith" the only true heresy, forever "dangerous to the soul."[17]

III

Less abrupt than it seems is the step from Cleombrotus, the
seeker of death, to the souls who have faced death in "the weeds
of Dominic / Or in *Franciscan* seek to pass disguis'd . . . at
Heav'ns Wicket." Forgetting that the motives for such shrouding
have varied all the way from gestures of respect for the orders
themselves to acts of attempted deception of the guardian of
Heaven by "the deluded mortals who hope to sneak into Heaven
by donning the garb of a monk,"[18] editors have usually cited
examples which they regarded as simply hypocritical, like those
of the poet Angelo Poliziano (d. 1494), who lay on his death-
bed in the Dominican habit, or of the Marquis Francesco Gon-
zaga (d. 1519), whose body first lay in state in his robes of
office and was later "clothed in the Franciscan habit, as he had
desired."[19] Examples multiply as late as that of the murdered
rightist leader, José Calvo Sotelo, whose body was buried in the
East Cemetery of Madrid, "draped in a monk's gown and habit,"
on the eve of the outbreak of the civil war in July, 1936.[20] But
the classical example is the case which Horrell mentions as traditional—that of Count Guido da Montefeltro, whom Dante meets

in the eighth circle of Hell[21] wearing the Franciscan habit which he had seriously assumed to repent his sins in his old age. At his death Guido says that St. Francis claimed his soul, but had to yield it to one of the black cherubs who justly accused him of having abetted Boniface VIII in a political crime after accepting the papal absolution for all his sins, both past and future.

Implicit in Guido's story are the "Indulgences, Dispenses, Pardons, Bulls" which are soon to become the "sport of winds" on "the backside of the World" in Milton's allegorical vision. They are specimens of the vanity which will vitiate human life after the Fall. Professor W. J. Grace has parallelled them closely[22] in a passage of Burton's *Anatomy of Melancholy*[23] which rises to something like universal satire of human nature. In a symbolic way Milton's lines have their universality. They are both more and less narrowly focussed in a sectarian way than they are commonly supposed to be. The "Eremites and Friars," the "Cowls, Hoods and Habits" are rightly traced most immediately to Ariosto's anticlericalism,[24] but more precisely they are traceable to Milton's old memories of his passionate pamphleteering against the Anglican bishops in his anti-episcopal tracts. The obvious link with them is through his translation in *Of Reformation in England*[25] of the verses in the *Orlando Furioso,* Canto xxxiv, where Ariosto "brings Astolfo, the English Knight up to the moone, where S. *John,* as he feignes, met him":

> And to be short, at last his guid him brings
> Into a goodly valley, where he sees
> A mighty masse of things strangely confus'd,
> Things that on earth were lost, or were abus'd.

Milton's target in *Of Reformation* was the increasing power of the English bishops. His object in bringing Astolfo's lunar adventure into his argument at all was to recall the traditional source of all ecclesiastical venality in the donation of Constantine. So in the passage which has been quoted in part he went on immediately to say: "And amongst these so abused things listen what he met *withal under the conduct of the* Evengelist*."* Again Milton translated four lines:

> Then past hee to a flowry Mountaine greene,
> Which once smelt sweet, now stinks so odiously;
> This was that gift (if you the truth will have)
> That *Constantine* to good *Sylvestro* gave.

For Milton's purpose in *Of Reformation* Ariosto's most important lines were these. For us who use Ariosto's passage as a key to Milton's Limbo, the reference to Constantine's endowment of the Church is less enlightening than is his unconscious betrayal in his Commonplace Book[26] of an impression made upon him earlier by Ariosto's image at the end of the stanza for the famous bequest. Such "Alms given after death," Milton thought it worth while to record for future reference, "Ariosto counts among the things lost and useless, which he represents as flying about the orbit of the moon without any profit to the givers."

In essence Milton's Paradise of Fools is far from being a counterpart of Ariosto's "mock-heroic, mock Dantesque voyage into disillusion," which Professor Thomas Greene regards[27] as "for many readers . . . the quintessence" of the *Orlando Furioso*. In the context of the *Orlando* as a whole and in that of Astolfo's visit to the moon, Milton's Limbo is distinctly antipathetic to Ariosto's tolerant satire of a "futility [in whose] cool tranquillity of meaninglessness the world of action is folly and the world of poetry appealing only if it admits of being an unreal game."

IV

In the search for an allegorical background resembling Milton's Paradise of Fools in essence as well as in literal detail, there is a clue in Greene's description of Astolfo's lunar experience as "mock-Dantesque." Independently of that suggestion, Professor Irene Samuel has pleaded[28] that Milton's allegory is imbued with the spirit of Dante's severe treatment of the souls whom he meets just inside Hell's gates before he reaches the Limbo of theological tradition where the noble pagans are found with Empedocles among them. Outside of the haunts of the philosophers are the souls of men who were blown about by every wind of doctrine without ever seriously committing themselves to any faith or cause. They are scorned alike by Mercy and Justice. They have been evaders of all commitment,

Che visser sanza infamia e sanza lodo.[29]

Having behaved like the angels who were neither for God nor for Satan in the war in Heaven, they are

A Dio spiacenti ed a' nemici sui[30]

—abominable to God and to his enemies alike.

Dante's image for the whirling mobs of the trimmers resembles the "violent cross wind" which Milton imagines driving the expectant applicants at "Heav'ns Wicket . . . transverse a thousand Leagues awry / Into the devious Air." Again the key image is violent wind. Dante's drifting multitudes are swept through the darkness like sand in a cyclone. Miss Samuel sees them as "mass-men" for whose "emptiness" Milton shares Dante's contempt. Because they "belong neither to the saved nor the damned, Dante puts them just within the gates [of Hell]. Milton puts them at the juncture of Chaos and cosmos." With perfect fidelity to his own nature, he doomed them to their wind-whipped agony because he shared with Dante the temperament to which Erich Auerbach attributed Dante's invention of the punishment of the souls unworthy of admission to Hell itself. Both men were "passionate, fearless, and indomitable in espousal of the good, and for whom active struggle was the natural form of life."

V

But the winds blowing in Milton's Limbo may have originated in the Socratic passage on the immortality of the souls of philosophers in the *Phaedo,* which so touched Cleombrotus. In "Milton's

Paradise of Fools,"[31] Professor E. L. Marilla traces them to
Socrates' denial that the winds beyond the tomb have any terrors
for himself or his friends: "Never fear, Simmias and Cebes, that
the soul which has been thus [philosophically] nurtured, . . . will
at her departure from the body be blown away by the winds, and
be nowhere, and nothing."[32] The image is implicit in Socrates'
entire argument, and was already all but explicit when he denied
that "the noble and wise soul on her way to the good and wise
God is blown away with the body, as the many say."[33]

The Platonic link here is corroborated by Mrs. J. W. Bennett's
earlier demonstration[34] of what may be regarded as the similar
cosmic localization of Milton's Limbo and the mysterious "meadow" of the vision of Er in the *Republic*. Both are mysterious
places on the edge of the universe where disembodied souls
sojourn. A connection of Plato's "meadow" with the Limbo
of medieval theology is brilliantly established as a part of Neoplatonic tradition by her translation of a passage from Marsilio
Ficino's Commentary on Er's vision. Ficino places it "between
the lower world and the heavens" and describes its character as
intermediate "between a good and evil state, . . . and between
bliss and misery." He explicitly describes it as "like a limbo in the
air" [*limbo similis in aere designatus*]. Of course, Plato's "meadow" has no violent winds, and its function in the Platonic cycle
of metempsychosis is incongruent with Christian and Miltonic
thought, but it is a place of more or less severe conditioning of
souls for rebirth. And it has one feature which almost certainly
sheds light upon Milton's express inclusion of "Embryo's and
Idiots" in his Limbo. Ficino says: "Likewise in such a meadow
reside longest—according to the Platonists—the souls of those
who die in infancy."

To "Idiots" it seems sound to apply the Miltonic definition of
the word in *Animadversions*:[35] "A learned fool in religion is an
idiot." "Embryo's" is probably best understood as meaning simply "infants." Marilla is inclined to think that it is used here with
direct reference to the Platonic passage, and with deliberate

involvement of the souls of infants with those of the builders of
Babel and all the other future denizens of his Limbo in the
common fate of "final dissolution." Yet, while it may be that
Milton is consciously denying his "Embryo's" the "perfect subjective happiness" which (according to the *Catholic Encyclope-
dia*)[36] has been consistently assigned to them by Catholics since
the time of St. Gregory of Nazianzen, it is obvious that Milton
was not condemning his "Embryo's" to absolute damnation. And
to make "final dissolution" apply to any human beings (regardless of age) would be in conflict with Milton's firm assertion of
the doctrine of the resurrection in *De Doctrina Christiana*, I,
XXXIII, and with Adam's final recognition that "to the faithful
death (is) the Gate of Life." (XII. 571).

With Marilla, we may agree that Milton deliberately leaves the
fate of both infants and all souls indistinctly good or bad un-
solved. For, "in any case," as he puts it, Milton "was not actually
committed to 'authoritative' pronouncement on an issue that did
not come within the framework of major emphasis in the
poem." But a better view of the entire passage sees it involved
with the vision of Er as Ficino interpreted it. Milton carefully
situates his Limbo, like Er's "meadow," on the outside of the
universe. It is not to be confused with Ariosto's lunar haunts of
human folly. The wanderers in Milton's Limbo are not to be found

> in the . . . Moon, as some have dream'd;
> Those argent Fields more likely habitants
> Translated Saints, or middle Spirits hold
> Betwixt th' Angelical and Human kind.

The best light on the "middle Spirits" who may inhabit the Moon
is Neoplatonic and comes from Tomasso Benci's interpretation of
Socrates' speech in the *Symposium* in Ficino's commentary.[37]
Quoting supporting passages from the *Phaedrus, Philebus,* and
Laws, as well as Socrates' speech in the *Symposium,* Benci (representing Ficino) explains "how the daemons inhabit the middle
ground between the heaven and earth." Among them are the

beings "which live in the region of ethereal fire located under the moon." Similar beings, it is true, are widely distributed in the regions between heaven and earth. Among them no "Translated Saints" are found, but Benci does declare that their inhabitants correspond to some of the orders of the angels, "Ministers of God." In the regions where these "middle Spirits" dwell there is no place for a Paradise of Fools. Of course, these regions would be equally inhospitable to the denizens of the valley of folly which Astolfo visited on Ariosto's moon.

By this time it should be clear that the only firmly identifiable "source" for Milton's Limbo of Fools is an imaginative conflation of scenes to which Plato and the Neoplatonists have contributed more, and Ariosto less, than has been supposed by most editors of *Paradise Lost*. In location and in some minor details the Platonic influences are obvious. And Plato seems to have been the begetter of Milton's image of the "violent cross wind" that blows the fools of his Paradise "transverse" from immediate disappointment to ultimate dissolution. But it was Dante who transformed the power of that image to something like the vivid physical force and moral propriety infusing it in both the *Commedia* and the epic.

University of Wisconsin

NOTES

1. In *The Spectator,* No. 297; 9 February, 1712.

2. *Paradise Lost,* II, 727–770.

3. *Lives of the Poets,* ed. G. B. Hill (Oxford, 1905), Vol. I, pp. 186–187.

4. In his edition of *Paradise Lost,* 1732.

5. In *Review of English Studies,* XVIII (1942), 413–427.

6. In *English Literary History,* XXI (1954), 107–113.

7. Berta Moritz-Siebeck in "Milton's 'Paradise of Fools,'" *Anglia,* 79 (1961), 153–176.

8. Genesis, 6. 2 and 4.

9. Other embroideries upon Jacob's vision are reviewed by C. A. Patrides in "Renaissance Interpretations of Jacob's Ladder." *Theologische Zeitschrift,* Jahrgang 18 (1962), 411–418.

10. *Paradise Regained* II, 179–180, alluding to Genesis 6. 2 and 4.

11. *English Studies,* XLII (1961), 159–164.

12. *Works of John Milton* (Columbia Edition), Vol. IV, p. 284.

13. IV Kings, 2. 11.

14. Callimachus, *Epigram* 25.

15. *Heaven Upon Earth & Characters of Vertues and Vices.* Ed. Rudolf Kirk (New Brunswick, N. J., 1958), 214.

16. Edited by A. B. Grosart from the holograph in the Harleian Collection (1879). Vol. II, pp. 163–164.

17. *Works,* IV, 284.

18. The words are Sir Herbert Grierson's in *Milton and Wordsworth* (Cambridge, 1937), p. 113.

19. Teste Julia Cartwright in *Isabella d'Este, Marchioness of Mantua* (New York, 1903), Vol. II, p. 156.

20. Teste Cecil C. Eby in *The Siege of the Alcazar* (New York, 1965), p. 23.

21. *Inferno,* XXVII, 16–132.

22. "Notes on Robert Burton and John Milton," *Studies in Philology* LII (1955), 590.

23. Everyman Edition, Vol. III, p. 333.

24. Howard Schultz, *Milton and Forbidden Knowledge* (New York, 1955), p. 126.

25. *Works,* III, 27.

26. *Works,* XVIII, 162.

27. In *The Descent from Heaven* (New Haven, 1963), p. 131.

28. In *Dante and Milton* (Ithaca, 1966), pp. 85–93. Writing independently in "Milton's Limbo of Vanity and Dante's Vestibule," in *English Language Notes,* III (1966), 177–182, Prof. Norma Phillips noted Dante's influence in Milton's wind imagery and in his conception of the inhabitants of his Limbo as men who "hanno perduto il ben dell' intelleto" (*Inferno,* III, 18).

29. *Inferno,* III, 36.

30. *Inferno,* III 63.

31. In *English Studies,* XLII (1961), 159–164.

32. *Dialogues of Plato,* translated by Benjamin Jowett (New York, 1871–1872), Vol. I, p. 432.

33. *Ibid.,* p. 428.

34. In "Milton's Use of the Vision of Er"; *Modern Philology,* XXXVI (1938–1939), 351–358. In "That Unnecessary Shell of Milton's World"—*Studies in Honor of T. W. Baldwin,* ed. Don Cameron Allen (Urbana, 1958), pp. 213–215—Professor Harry F. Robins points out some resemblances between the cosmic situation of Milton's Limbo and the "good land" beyond the universe which Origen describes in *De Principiis* as the temporary residence of imperfect souls. In spite of radical differences between that luminous, calm region and Milton's Limbo, Robins regards "Origen's purgatory [as] trenchantly satirized in the Miltonic passage."

35. *Works,* V, 165.

36. Vol. IX, pp. 258.2–259.1.

37. The quotation is from Sears Jayne's translation of Ficino's Commentary on the *Symposium* (Columbia, Missouri, 1944), pp. 184–185.

THE HERESIES OF SATAN

William B. Hunter, Jr.

No critical observation can seem more platitudinous than that
Milton conceived Satan as a heretic, though in our own age,
which has had its share of critical platitudes, no one seems to
have uttered it. There is indeed solid ecclesiastical sanction for
viewing Satan as the source of heresies: 1 Timothy 4:1 asserts
that "in the latter times some shall depart from the faith, giving
heed to seducing spirits, and doctrines of devils." Eusebius interprets half-a-dozen heresies as having originated in this way,[1] and
the most extensive ancient account of them, written by Epiphanius
in the Fourth Century, is entitled *Panarion*—that is, the *Medicine
Chest,* composed of antidotes for those bitten by the serpent of
heresy.[2]

Milton's depiction of the heretical nature of his great Antagonist is remarkably subtle; indeed, many critics have found Satan
so persuasive that they have supported his point of view. Comparison with Marlowe's method of characterization in *Dr. Faustus* is revealing. Agent of the devil though he is, Mephistophilis
speaks blasphemy but does not himself believe it at all. For
instance, he demonstrably holds the major Christian tenet, faith
in the Trinity, because he advises Faustus that the shortest way to
conjure is "stoutly to abjure the Trinity" (I, iii, 53)—scarcely a
denial of the existence of the Trinity or of its importance. In the

25

same way Marlowe's Lucifer is never in doubt about the existence of Christ or about Christ's righteousness: "Christ," he advises, "cannot save thy soul, for he is just" (II, ii, 85). Mephistophilis is indistinguishable from a Christian minister when he counsels Faustus in horror to "leave these frivolous demands / Which strike a terror to my fainting soul" (I, iii, 81–2). Marlowe's devils must indeed be the most orthodox of beings, for if they should deny for themselves any orthodox belief they would be, so to speak, out of business in that they derive their reality and reason for existence solely from their opposition to God, in whose being they must accordingly have the greatest faith.

Milton's Satan is just as fundamentally opposed to God, but he is pictured in a very different and far more subtle way, expounding his heretical views without any indication to the reader that they are unorthodox. The naive reader may not even be aware of the significance of what he reads because Milton assumes for his fit though small audience a grounding in Christian fundamentals which will lead it to immediate recognition of the heresies which are being implied.

To begin with one of the more obvious points, one should observe that throughout *Paradise Lost* Satan does not really believe in God's omnipotence and bows before him only because he has been beaten in battle. All of his acts furthermore imply denial of God's omnipresence and omniscience as well; especially ironic, because it is so fruitless, is his stay on the dark side of the earth so as to escape detection of God's agent Uriel before he tempts Eve. The entire debate in hell is built on the same delusion (one which Eve shares after her own fall when she wonders whether God has seen her deed, IX, 811 ff.) Furthermore, Satan and his followers are without exception fatalists who appeal on every occasion to fate as being superior to God, in contrast to Christian freedom as well as to God's express statement, "Necessity and Chance / Approach not mee, and what I will is Fate" (VII, 172–3).[3]

As has long been recognized, Satan, Sin, and Death are a parody of the Christian Trinity, but even this unholy group is debased by the fact that Satan and all of the devils are polytheists, considering each other to be "gods."[4] They, however, never undergo such union as Christianity expounds of the Godhead, for the Trinity are mystically united.[5] Furthermore, regenerate Christians unite with Christ and he in turn with the Father so that at last "God shall be all in all" (III, 341; VI, 732; XI, 44). Representing the idea of union in yet another way is the coalescence of the good angels into one body as the Son overwhelms Satan in heaven: they are "circumfus'd on either Wing, / Under their Head imbodied all in one" (VI, 778–9). The evil angels, on the other hand, are never united into one body, mystical or otherwise. They fight as individuals and they fall as individuals, in resolute pluralism.[6]

In yet another example of union, again a faulty one, Satan unwillingly but unconsciously parodies the Incarnation when in Book IX he joins himself with the serpent in order to tempt Eve. This union must be understood quite otherwise from his earlier appearances in the guise of a cormorant (IV, 196), of various four-footed beasts including the lion and tiger (IV, 397 ff.), and of a toad by Eve's ear (IV, 800). On none of these occasions does he unite his being with that of another: he is merely *like* a toad, just as in Book X the devils assume the shapes of serpents without being joined with other creatures. But in Book IX Satan must "incarnate and imbrute" his essence in union with an animal, a union accomplished with the greatest reluctance and to be contrasted with the Son's voluntary union with man in order to save the human race (III, 236–40) as Mary Pecheux has well remarked.[7] But Christ's union with man is imperishable, whereas Satan's ends as soon as the temptation is over and he resumes his usual form so as to observe the outcome (X, 333–4).[8]

In many ways Milton's most fundamental, if subtle, depiction of deviation from orthodoxy lies in Satan's attitude towards the Son of God. I wish to begin consideration of this area of his

heresy with the acute observation by C. A. Patrides that in
Paradise Lost Satan consistently refuses to allude in any way
whatsoever to the existence of the Son and that the other fallen
angels likewise resolutely avoid any mention of him.[9] The fact is
especially surprising, as Patrides notes, in view of the undoubted
fact that the exaltation of the Son precipitated this rebellion in
heaven and that the Son himself was the sole instrument in the
defeat of the forces of evil described in Book VI. This exclusion
of the Son from all discussion of the events is too complete to be
accidental. In Satan's terms, God defeated him "with his Thunder" (I, 93), and indeed only this thunder has made him greater
than Satan (I, 258). Mammon remembers being overcome by a
"fierce Foe" (II, 78), an evasion repeated in Satan's epithet
"Almighty Foe" (II, 769). Although in *Paradise Lost* Satan
never suggests that the Son exists in any sense, Milton as in-
terpretive author can say, of course, that the motive of the war in
heaven derived from "envy against the Son of God" (V, 662).

In having Satan ignore the very existence of the Son, Milton
almost inevitably had in mind one of the earliest heresies to arise
in the church, monarchianism. It was particularly insidious because monarchianism had originally been advanced to under-
score the unity of the Christian Trinity: the earliest church fathers argued that the Godhead acts as a unit, that it is a single
rule, a *mon-arch*. Such, for instance, was the position of the
orthodox Justin Martyr, who had composed a treatise, now lost,
On the Sole Government (μοναρχία) *of God*. Milton himself
employs this orthodox sense to state that Satan fought against
"the Throne and Monarchy of God" (I, 42)—that is, against the
Godhead. But as Tertullian sadly observed, Satan sometimes
destroys the truth by defending it. Accordingly, Satan "maintains
that there is only one Lord, the Almighty Creator of the world, in
order that out of this doctrine of the unity he may fabricate a
heresy."[10] From the orthodox monarchianism of a unified rule,
heretics who overstressed the unity of God developed monarchianism to mean a single god rather than the single rule of a

triune Godhead. The word *monarchian* quickly became synonymous with denial of the independent existence of the Son or of the divinity of Christ for which Tertullian attacked Praxeas, Hippolytus attacked Noetus, and Athanasius attacked Paul of Samosata. The issue continued at least until the time of Augustine, who confesses that before his conversion he regarded Christ as being merely "a perfect man," to be admired for his "certain great excellency of human nature and a more perfect participation of wisdom" but no more—not "the Word made flesh."[11]

Milton conceived Satan as a monarchian in the heretical sense of the word. Very early in the epic Satan asserts that God "reigns / Monarch in Heav'n" (I, 637–8). Before the war in heaven breaks out, he inveighs against a "Monarchy over such as live by right / His [God's] equals" (V, 795–6), an argument vigorously rebutted by Abdiel (V, 831 ff.). Sometimes the word is translated "Sole King" (II, 325) or tyrant (I, 124; II, 59; X, 466). From the perspective of the monarchian heresy, which denied that the Son was divine or even existed as a separate being, it is not at all surprising that Satan fails to make any mention of him. On the other hand, Satan is himself described in monarchian terms, complementary to his own stand relating to the Trinity (see, for instance, II, 428; II, 467; X, 375).

Scholars today distinguish two different forms of monarchianism. The earlier, termed "dynamic" monarchianism, is associated with two men named Theodotus (active about 200 A.D.), a Roman named Artemon, and especially Paul of Samosata, Bishop of Antioch.[12] Dynamic monarchianism considered the Logos to be merely a mode of activity of the one God, the Monarch, a "circumscription" whereby God by limiting himself reveals himself to man through some form of activity. From this viewpoint the Logos is "identical with the Father, having no personal existence of his own but only the 'circumscription' [that is, the self-limitation] of the Father."[13] As Eusebius quotes the monarchian statement of one Beryllus, Bishop of Bostra in Arabia, the Son "before his incarnation, had no being according unto

the circumscription (περιγραφή) of a proper and severed substance, and . . . had no proper divinity, but only his fathers
divinity, dwelling in himselfe."[14] The Son, that is, is only a phase
of the activity of the Father. In contrast, Justin Martyr had
earlier argued a more orthodox view that the Word had originated as an independent being from the undiminished, the uncir-
cumscribed, being of the Father: "God begat before all creatures
a Beginning, who was a certain rational power proceeding from
Himself. . . . He was begotten of the Father by an act of will
. . . , yet not by abscission, so as to lessen the word"—that is,
the reasoning power of the Father. The uttered Logos then exists
"by itself, not diminishing that from which it was kindled."[15]
Milton expresses the same anti-monarchian view that the Father
is not diminished or circumscribed when at the creation the
Father proclaims:

> I am who fill
> Infinitude, nor vacuous the space
> Though I uncircumscrib'd myself retire,
> And put not forth my goodness, which is free
> To act or not.   (VII, 168–72)

The second form of monarchianism is usually entitled "Modalistic"; it is associated with the names of Praxeas, Noetus, and
especially Sabellius. According to this second conception, the
Son indeed exists but only as a different mode of appearance of
the Father, who now reveals himself as the Son and who in time
is born of Mary and dies as Christ. Because this modalistic
monarchianism argued that God died in the form of Christ its
devotees are also called patripassians.

Examination of *Paradise Lost* alone does not clearly reveal
which of the two forms of monarchianism—dynamic or modalistic—Milton had in mind as he depicted Satan, for the distinction
is not drawn clearly by monarchians themselves until the Incara-
tion occurs. It is necessary, therefore, to turn to *Paradise Regained* in order to complete this consideration of how Milton

conceived of Satan's monarchianism. In the later poem the devil at once identifies God in traditional monarchian terms: "He who obtains the Monarchy of Heav'n" will stop at nothing to help his Son get ahead (I, 87–8). In this poem, of course, Satan must acknowledge the existence of the Son as an actual being, in contrast with his attitude in *Paradise Lost* which has already been stated. With such recognition, which form of monarchianism does he espouse? As Tertullian argues, the modalistic monarchian will interpret the temptation in the wilderness, the subject of *Paradise Regained,* as being addressed to the Father himself, not to a separate Son. According to such misinformed people Satan believed that "it was God Himself that I approached; it was the Almighty Himself that I tempted face to face" (*Against Praxeas,* 1). *Paradise Regained,* however, yields no evidence that Satan thought that he was tempting the Father.

The alternative for a monarchian is the "dynamic" view that Satan thinks that he is addressing merely the man Jesus. As Eusebius observed, Paul of Samosata held "low and degraded views of Christ, namely, that in his nature he was a common man."[16] This is Satan's view in *Paradise Regained.* Accordingly, he denies the significance of baptism (I, 73), and refuses to believe that Jesus embodies the being who he now admits defeated him in heaven (I, 89–90). In the same vein he fails to understand the meaning of the appearance of the dove which announced that Jesus was Son of God (I, 83 ff.). As he later observes, in Jesus is

> united
> What of perfection can in man be found,
> Or human nature can receive   (III, 229–31)

but no more—the same view as that of Augustine before his conversion when, as has been seen, he was under the sway of the monarchian heresy. Likewise in the final temptation Satan still doubts that Christ is "Son of God" in any divine sense. After all, he argues, "Son of God" may mean any being at all:

The Son of God I also am, or was,
And if I was, I am; relation stands;
All men are Sons of God. (IV, 518–20)

Such is the view of dynamic monarchianism as applied to Jesus, who for Satan is accordingly "th'utmost of mere man . . . , Not more" (IV, 535–6). His amazement at his complete failure in the temptations is both theologically and dramatically justified.

An especially interesting sidelight appears in the temptation of classical learning which Satan put before Jesus (IV, 221 ff.). Because of Milton's own firm grounding in this subject, commentators have been baffled by Christ's immediate rejection of this temptation. First he asserts that he already knows the material (IV, 286–8), and then he proceeds to show its shortcomings in comparison with the revelation of scripture. It has not been generally recognized that there is strong ecclesiastical support for his stand: that classical philosophy was considered by some to be a fertile source of heresy. Such is the judgment of Greek culture forcefully expressed in Book I of Hippolytus' *Refutation of All Heresies,* which was available to Milton,[17] and in Epiphanius' *Panarion,* which as has been shown Milton certainly knew. The condemnation of Greek thought as heretical by these early Christians does not, of course, make Christ's condemnation of it any more palatable to modern humanists, but Milton himself was a Christian before he was a humanist.

If Milton were consciously picturing Satan as a heretic of the dynamic monarchian persuasion, as has been argued here, one final observation should be made. This particular heresy denies that the Son has any individual existence and accordingly that Christ is in any sense divine. As all historians of early Christian thought have observed, such a view led in time to the full-blown Arianism which the Council of Nicaea condemned. If, that is, Milton were an Arian as many have argued, he is just as certainly of the devil's party as he depicts that party in *Paradise Lost* and

Paradise Regained. Blake and Shelley were right about Milton's views in a deeper sense than has hitherto been realized.

Macalester College

NOTES

1. See, for instance, his *Ecclesiastical History,* III, 26, 27; IV, 7; V, 14, conveniently available in *Nicene and Post-Nicene Fathers,* 2nd Series, I.

2. *Patrologiae Graecae,* XLI; never translated into English. Milton knew the work well enough to refer to it several times.

3. The observation goes back as far as Bishop Newton. For a systematic discussion see Ben Gray Lumpkin, "Fate in *Paradise Lost,*" *SP,* XLIV (1947), 56–68.

4. See J. C. Maxwell, " 'Gods' in 'Paradise Lost,' " *N&Q,* CXCIII (1948), 234–42.

5. Probably parodied in the experience of Sin when in Hell she experiences an attractive power from Satan on Earth which she describes as a "connatural force / Powerful at greatest distance to unite / With secret amity things of like kind" (X, 246–8).

6. For a discussion of various kinds of union, see my "Milton on the Incarnation: Some More Heresies," *JHI,* XXI (1960), 349 ff.

7. "O Foul Descent!': Satan and the Serpent Form," *SP,* LXII (1965), 188–96. Satan enters the serpent through its mouth (IX, 187). It is not clear whether this is a parody of the traditional incarnation through Mary's ear.

8. See "Milton on the Incarnation," pp. 356–7.

9. "The Godhead in *Paradise Lost:* Dogma or Drama?," *JEGP,* LXIV (1965), 32. As a matter of fact, he never names God the Father, calling him one or another opprobrious epithet. But he does admit the Father's existence.

10. *Against Praxeas,* 1, in *Ante-Nicene Fathers,* III, 597.

11. *Confessions,* VII, 19, in *Nicene and Post-Nicene Fathers,* 1st Series, I, 113.

12. Ancient authorities are Epiphanius, already cited, Eusebius, *Ecclesiastical History,* especially V, 28, quoting the anonymous "Little Labyrinth" and Athanasius *de Synodis* 26. For a modern analysis see J. F. Bethune-Baker, *An Introduction to the Early History of Christian Doctrine* (London, 1962), pp. 98 ff.

13. Bethune-Baker, p. 99.

14. *Ecclesiastical History*, VI, xxxii (i.e., xxxiii), quoted from Meredith Hanmer's translation (London, 1636, 4th edition), p. 111.

15. *Dialogue with Trypho*, 61, in *Ante-Nicene Fathers*, I, 227.

16. *Ecclesiastical History*, VII, 27, in *Post-Nicene Fathers*, 2nd Series, I, 312.

17. See *Ante-Nicene Fathers*, V.

THE COMPOSITION OF MILTON'S *DE DOCTRINA CHRISTIANA*—THE FIRST STAGE

Maurice Kelley

Of the stages by which he composed the *De Doctrina Christiana,* Milton has left a brief account in the preface to his treatise.[1] The first stage began while he was still a boy with his study of the Old and New Testaments in their original languages, and ended with his perusal of certain shorter systems of divinity and his institution of a commonplace book, where following their example, he collected under general headings scriptural passages that might prove useful on later occasions.[2] The second stage Milton initiated with his study of more voluminous treatises and their discussions of certain disputed heads of faith; and his own systematic theology grew out of his disappointment with these works. Their frequent errors and intellectual dishonesties made them unsafe guides to salvation; and since Milton believed that he must have a reliable guide, or at least an honest attempt at one, he compiled a guide of his own making—his *De Doctrina Christiana . . . Disquisitionum Libri Duo.*

In general, Milton's account accords with what we can learn

elsewhere about his early language studies. *The Reason of Church Government* contains Milton's report that he was "exercis'd to the tongues" from his "first yeeres";[3] "Ad Patrem," 11. 81–85, indicates that these tongues included Hebrew and Greek; Letter 1, to Thomas Young, conveys Milton's thanks to his former tutor for the "Hebrew Bible, your very welcome gift";[4] and recent studies[5] indicate that this linguistic training was quite in accord with the seventeenth century grammar school curriculum, and differed from it, in Milton's case, only in greater breadth and depth.

Similarly, the making of commonplace books was a method of assembling material taught in Renaissance grammar schools, and one frequently employed by incipient students of divinity.[6] No theological notebook by Milton has come down to us, but eleven entries in the surviving *Commonplace Book* refer to a lost "Index Theologicus"[7] that contained at least 42 pages,[8] and had headings on Church, Church Goods, Councils, Idolatry, Pope, and Religion not to be Forced.[9] Ten of these references are in Milton's hand; and where evidence for dating occurs, they seem to have been entered from about 1640 to 1646 or later.[10] The eleventh reference is in the hand of Milton's nephew, Edward Phillips, and may be provisionally dated between November, 1651 and February, 1652.[11]

Also belonging to the 1640's is a second theological endeavor by Milton, which Edward Phillips[12] reports of thus:

> The next work after this [for Milton's pupils on Sunday], was the writing from his own dictation, some part, from time to time, of a Tractate which he thought fit to collect from the ablest of Divines, who had written of that subject; *Amesius, Wollebius,* &c. *viz.* A perfect System of Divinity, of which more hereafter.

Despite this terminal promise, however, Phillips' *Life* says nothing further of this tractate; and like the "Index Theologicus," it has not come down to us.

From this first stage in the composition of the *De Doctrina,* then, we have no surviving documents—only evidence for lost work: a collection of scriptural passages referred to in the preface to the *De Doctrina*; an "Index Theologicus" inferred from cross references in the *Commonplace Book;* and a derivative theology, "A perfect System of Divinity," reported in Phillips' *Life.* Milton's account of how he composed the *De Doctrina,* however, mentions only one work; so our task in tracing the composition of Milton's treatise through its first stage is to determine—if possible—whether these three lost works were really three, two, or only one, referred to in three different ways.

To do so, we may begin with the "Index Theologicus," which does not seem to be the collection of scriptural passages referred to in Milton's preface. Its linkage, by cross reference, to the Ethical, Economic, and Political Indexes that constitute Milton's preserved *Commonplace Book* suggests that it was—as its name indicates—"another index," and like the other three consisted of notes on secular reading rather than of biblical quotations. Its headings—Church Goods, Councils, Pope, and Religion not to be Forced—seem unlikely ones for the collection of proof texts, for they suggest temporal aspects of the church—administrative and political—and Milton in the *De Doctrina* finds no scriptural authority for Councils and Popes, and documents his discussion of Religion not to be Forced with only two proof texts.[13]

"A perfect System of Divinity," however, may well have been the collection of which Milton speaks in his preface; but to establish this likelihood, we must temporarily leave these lost works to consider certain sources of the *De Doctrina—the Medulla SS. Theologiæ* of Guilielmus Amesius and the *Compendium Theologiæ Christianæ* of Johannes Wollebius, which were also, according to Phillips, sources of "A perfect System."

For Milton's indebtedness to these two short treatises, let us consider the first two chapters of the *De Doctrina* (I, i–ii). Here, Milton's reason for writing his theological work is similar to that given by Amesius.[14] Milton, like Amesius, divides his work into two books; and his proof texts for this division and his observation that the two parts are in practice really one, both seem to draw on the *Medulla*.[15] Amesius' recourse to *anthropopatheia* probably prompted in part at least Milton's disclaimer of the figure;[16] and other similarities to Amesius in I, i–ii appear in Milton's remarks on man's inability to apprehend God,[17] on God's nature being indefinable,[18] on God's attributes showing who and what he is,[19] on God's power not being exercised in anything that involves a contradiction,[20] and on the sources of God's perfection.[21]

In this same section of the *De Doctrina* similarities to Wollebius' *Compendium* are likewise evident. Some of these are the definition of Christian doctrine,[22] the use of 2 Timothy 1:13—and in the Greek—to sanction compilation of systems of divinity,[23] and the observations that God is known in himself and in his works,[24] and through his names and his properties,[25] that his names show either his nature or his power,[26] that the name "Jehovah" signifies not only God's nature but also His promises and their fulfillment,[27] and that the plural form "Elohim" may have a singular meaning.[28] Other similarities concern the meanings of the other names of God,[29] the etymology of "Jehovah,"[30] the eternity of God,[31] and his attributes of life, intellect, and will.[32]

Such, then, are the chief similarities between these two "ablest of divines" and Milton in the first two chapters of his *De Doctrina Christiana;* and if we extract from these chapters matters added later to buttress the antitrinitarianism found today in chapters v–vi,[33] we are left with a set of theological topics that may be aptly described as having been collected from "Amesius, Wollebius, &c.,"[34] and ordered after their patterns.

For further evidence of this ordering, consider Milton's dependence on Wollebius in Book II of the *De Doctrina*. In both it and the *Compendium,* the second book consists of two parts: the Duties of Man to God and the Duties of Man to Man. In the first part, chapters i–iii of both treatises are similarly organized: the general virtues are identical and most of the special external virtues and their opposing vices are the same, with the correspondences often showing close verbal agreement. For instance:

Compendium, II, iii, p. 192	*De Doctrina,* II, iii; XVII, 60
Timor Dei est, quo Dei Verbum & Majestatem sic reveremur, ut offensam tam benigni Patris omnibus modis præcaveamus, non tam pœnæ formidine quam Dei amore. . . . Huic opponitur Securitas Carnalis, Timor servilis, & Timor idololatricus.	TIMOR Dei est quo Deum sicut summum patrem omnium et iudicem reveremur, eiusque offensionem summe timemus. . . . Huic opponitur securitas carnalis. . . . Et timor servilis. . . . Et idololatricus.

In chapters iv–vi, the virtues and vices are in general the same, and significant verbal parallelism continues. In the second part of Book II, Milton's organization differs from that of the corresponding part of Wollebius; but in varying degrees, *De Doctrina* viii is similar to *Compendium* viii and xiv; *DD* ix to *C* xi–xii; *DD* x to *C* iii; *DD* xi to *C* viii; *DD* xii to *C* x; *DD* xiii to *C* xiii; *DD* xiv to *C* xii; while *DD* xv–xvii seem expansions of certain parts of *C* ix, x, xii.

Both "A perfect System" and the *De Doctrina,* then, have close connections with the shorter systematic theologies of Amesius and Wollebius. "A perfect System," according to Phillips, was collected out of "Amesius, Wollebius, &c."; and the three preceding paragraphs of this study indicate that the *De Doctrina* derives much in form and content from these same theologians. Not unreasonable, therefore, would be the conclusion that the Amesius-Wollebius materials present in the *De Doctrina* arrived there *via* "A perfect System," and that "A perfect System" constituted the primary version of the *De Doctrina.*

Equally not unreasonable seems a second conclusion—that "A perfect System" is also the collection of scriptural passages that Milton speaks of in the *De Doctrina.* His preface mentions only one work, the collection; and that work he connected with

"Theologorum Systemata aliquot breviora . . . ad eorum . . . exemplum" he set up "locos communes" and assembled scriptural passages under them. "A perfect System" and the *De Doctrina* likewise have connections with some of the shorter systems; so if we combine our two conclusions—making the collection and "A perfect System" one and the same work, and that work the primary version of the *De Doctrina*—then we can trace the *De Doctrina*—as Milton does—to a single work, where the theological topics were collected from "Amesius, Wollebius, &c." with Milton's contribution consisting, for the most part, in the collection of more proof texts. Such a situation will explain numerous portions of the *De Doctrina,* such as the following, where Milton has merely restated Amesius or Wollebius and added further documentation:

Medulla, I, iv, 66, p. 23.	*De Doctrina,* I, ii; XIV, 60.
Ex istis omnibus attributis resultat illa Dei perfectio ex qua dicitur *beatus.* I Timoth. 1.11. & 6. 15. 67. Hinc fides nostra firmum habet fundamentum; quia nititur Deo, omnis perfectionis, beatitudinis, & gloriæ possessore, & autore.	Ex his omnibus attributis efflorescit illa summa Dei excellentia qua vere est perfectus, et in summa gloria vere beatus, et iure quidem summo et merito suo dominus omnium supremus, ut passim nominatur. Psal. xvi. 11. *satietas gaudiorum in conspectu tuo.* et civ. 1. *gloriam et maiestatem induisti.* Dan. vii. 10. *cui millies mille ministrabant.* Matt. v. 48. *sicut pater perfectus est.* I Tim. 1. 11. *beatus Deus.* et vi. 15. *ille beatus.*

If the method employed thus far is sound, then we can add some details to Milton's spare account of the initial stage in his composition of the *De Doctrina.* Milton's early studies produced two works, now lost, on religion. One, to which he frequently referred in the 1640's, was his "Index Theologicus," a companion to the Ethical, Economic, and Political Indexes that make up his extant *Commonplace Book*. Its known headings suggest that it derived its notes from non-biblical sources, was concerned with temporal aspects of the church, and contributed little, if anything, to the completed *De Doctrina*.[35] The second work was that called by Phillips "A perfect System of Divinity." Just when Milton began to "collect" it, we do not know;[36] but by the mid-1640's it had reached a state of completeness where Phillips could call it a "Tractate," and its title indicates that it was not a notebook, like the "Index Theologicus," but a systematic theology. In compiling it, Milton worked as Erasmus had advised. He set up his theological *loci* by adopting "someone's collections," in this case, those of Amesius and Wollebius; and his own contribution consisted largely in assembling proof texts under their topics. If the documentation of the completed *De Doctrina* may be taken as indication of Milton's labors, he performed his work with diligence;[37] and the result was a short treatise heavily documented with proof texts and orthodox in dogma, which was to be converted during the next decade or so into the heterodox work now called the *De Doctrina Christiana*.

Princeton University

NOTES

1. For the complete Latin text of this account, see *The Works of John Milton* (Columbia Edition), XIV, 4–8.

2. "Coepi igitur Adolescens . . . cum ad libros utriusque Testamenti lingua sua perlegendos assiduus incumbere, tum Theologorum Systemata aliquot breviora sedulo percurrere: ad eorum deinde exemplum, locos communes digerere, ad quos omnia quæ ex scripturis haurienda occurrissent, expromenda cum opus esset, referrem" (XIV, 4, 10–17).

3. *Complete Prose Works of John Milton* (New Haven, 1953) I, 808–09, and *Second Defence, Complete Prose*, IV, 612–13.

4. *Complete Prose,* I, 312.

5. Donald L. Clark, *John Milton at St. Paul's School* (New York, 1948); Harris F. Fletcher, *The Intellectual Development of John Milton,* II (Urbana, 1961). Milton's training is possibly reflected in that proposed in *Of Education* and in that meted out to his own students. *Of Education* tells us that "ere this time the Hebrew tongue at a set hour might have been gain'd, that the Scriptures may be now read in their own originall; whereto it would be no impossibility to adde the *Chaldey,* and the *Syrian* dialect" (*Complete Prose,* II, 400). Of the language study of Milton's students, Edward Phillips writes: "Nor did the time thus Studiously imployed in conquering the *Greek* and *Latin* Tongues, hinder the attaining of the chief Oriental Languages, *viz.* The *Hebrew, Caldee,* and *Syriac,* so far as to go through the *Pentateuch* or Five Books of *Moses* in Hebrew, to make a good entrance into the *Targum,* or *Chaldee* Paraphrase, and to understand several Chapters of St. *Matthew* in the *Syriac* Testament" (*The Early Lives of John Milton,* ed. Helen Darbishire [London, 1932], p. 60–61).

6. Erasmus, for instance, in his *Ratio seu Methodus Compendio Perveniendi ad Veram Theologiam* (tr. from *Opera* [Basel, 1540], V, 110) under "Prepare theological *loci*" advises, "that you should either prepare some theological *loci* for yourself, or else adopt someone's collections: according to these, as pigeon holes, you should distribute all your selections, so that it may be easy where to see what you want to take out or file away, as for example, Faith, Fasting, Enduring Evils, . . . Study of Scripture, . . . and the like: for countless topics can be made up. When these have been arranged by conflicting or congruent content, as I pointed out earlier in my *Copia,* there should be put with them whatever is in any way remarkable in all the books of the Old Testament, Gospels, Acts, and Epistles, either agreeing or contradicting. If one wishes he may add from the ancient commentators, and even from the Gentiles, what he thinks may be useful. I believe that I can see from his own words that the divine Jerome used this system." For the practice of William Gouge, who died in 1653, see Samuel Clark's *Lives* (quoted Fletcher, *Intellectual Development,* II, 289): "In the first year of his Fellowship he began his *Commonplace* book for *Divinity,* in which he made references of all which he read. He also had white paper bound betwixt every leaf of his Bible, wherein he wrote such short and pithy interpretations, and observations on the Text as could not well be referred to any head in his Common place Book."

7. "Vide Indicem Theologicum" and "in indice altero," *Commonplace Book,* pp. 197, 221; *Complete Prose,* I, 477, 484.

8. "Vide Papa [pag.] 42," *Commonplace Book,* p. 221; *Complete Prose,* I, 484.

9. *Commonplace Book,* pp. 183, 244, 246, 12, 109 ("vide titul. de

bonis Ecclesiasticis"), 112, 183, 246, 221, 197; *Complete Prose,* I, 449, 501, 504, 365, 402, 407, 444, 504, 484, 477. Though noting it earlier (I, 365), *Complete Prose* (I, 501) omits the reference "vide Ecclesia," which should follow the citation "Hist. Concil. Trident 1. 2. p. 179." (11. 9–10), and for "p. 179" prints "p. 170," though the correct page number appears in the footnote below.

10. For probable dates of some of these entries, see footnotes in *Complete Prose,* I, on pages listed above in footnote 9 and James Holly Hanford, "The Chronology of Milton's Private Studies," *PMLA,* XXXVI (1921), 251–314.

11. *Commonplace Book,* p. 197; *Complete Prose,* I, 477. For date of this entry, see Maurice Kelley, "Milton and Machiavelli's *Discorsi,*" *SB,* IX (1951–52), 123–27.

12. Darbishire, *Early Lives,* p. 61. Masson (*Life,* III, 253, 656) dates Milton's period of teaching from 1639 to 1647.

13. Columbia, XVI, 228, 310; XVII, 394.

14. Columbia, XIV, 2, 7–10; Amesius, *Medulla* (Amsterdam, 1627), "Præmunitio Brevis," [*4].

15. XIV, 22, 11–24, 6; *Medulla,* I, ii, 1–4, pp. 5–6.

16. XIV, 32, 6; *Medulla,* I, iv, 4–6, pp. 14–15.

17. XIV, 30, 17; *Medulla,* I, iv, 2–3, p. 14.

18. XIV, 38, 8–10; *Medulla,* I, iv, 32, p. 19.

19. XIV, 40, 14; *Medulla,* I, iv, 31, p. 19.

20. XIV, 48, 7–9; *Medulla,* I, vi, 17, p. 35.

21. XIV, 60, 1–8; *Medulla,* I, iv, 66, p. 23.

22. XIV, 16, 1–4; Wollebius, *Compendium* (London, 1760), "Præcognita," p. 1.

23. XIV, 20, 14–15; *Compendium,* "Præfatio," p. iii.

24. XIV, 30, 4–5; *Compendium,* I, i, p. 8.

25. XIV, 38, 10–12; *Compendium,* I, i, p. 8.

26. XIV, 38, 13–14; *Compendium,* I, i, p. 9.

27. XIV, 40, 5–8; *Compendium,* I, i, p. 9.

28. XIV, 52, 15–17; *Compendium,* I, i, p. 9.

29. XIV, 38, 14–24; *Compendium,* I, i, p. 9.

30. XIV, 38, 24–25; *Compendium,* I, i, p. 9.

31. XIV, 42, 14–16; *Compendium,* I, i, p. 11.

32. XIV, 54, 2–4; *Compendium,* I, i, p. 11.

33. For instance, Milton's interpretation of Heb. 1:3, his definition of eternity, his argument that God is not *actus purus,* and his elaborate discussion of the unity of God, XIV, 40, 42, 48–52.

34. Probably to be included in Phillips' "&c" are Amandus Polanus and Simon Episcopius. For Bishop Sumner's note on theologies that Milton must have known, see XVII, 575–76.

35. Possibly matter in the "Index Theologicus" under the heading Religion not to be Forced passed over into Milton's discussion of the duties of the magistrate in *De Doctrina,* II, xvii; XVII, 394 ff.

36. In *Life Records* (I, 95–96), J. Milton French places "Studies theological works and makes theological notebook" under April, 1625; but his subsequent remarks furnish no documentation for such a precise date.

37. For instance, in the two passages on *Timor Dei* and its opposites quoted above, the original, Wollebius version has one proof text, Milton's version thirty; and in contrast to the sparse documentation of the second book of the *Compendium,* some three-fifths of that portion of the *De Doctrina* are proof texts.

MILTON AS SATIRIST
AND WIT

Edward Le Comte

With the Milton industry being only less than the Shakespeare industry, and the scraping—sometimes the rescraping—of the bottom of the barrel being heard in numerous parts of the groves of academe, it is surprising there has not been a book on Milton as satirist and wit.[1] The materials are on hand, with annotations, and they are timely. One may even experience on this tercentenary a nostalgia for a strong trait and talent ordinarily passed over as a weakness about which the less said the better. Milton! thou shouldst be living at this hour, not as a soul dwelling apart but as a fighter in the arena. The age "hath need of thee"—because it needs a satirist. Mary McCarthy, William F. Buckley, Jr., and acid reviews and letters in the *Times Literary Supplement* do not quite suffice. Ours is the age of, above all, smooth interpersonal relations, other-directed timidity, the fear of offending, at least with words. It is impolite—and most undemocratic—to have style. In public one does not rumble (that now connotes riots); one mumbles. Our insecure aversion to "sharp, but saving words"[2] is such that we do not care to pay the price, in wounds, of being saved.

However, enough of beating one's own times, pleasurable though that tends to be: let us rather examine how Milton beat his. Admittedly he composed no formal satires, unless a half-dozen epigrams in Latin or Greek count as such. (E. K. Rand thought that "In Quintum Novembris" came close: "one of the most powerful of his poems, . . . but in structure it is an epyllion, a mock-epyllion, rather than satire."[3]) Yet the very recent critic who goes so far as to say, "the comic forms expressing satirical and ironic themes, he [Milton] found uncongenial," has to qualify by mentioning in the next sentence the Hobson poems, and complicates the issue by referring later to "the antimasque of grotesque deities" in the Nativity Ode and the section of "demonic parody" in *Comus.*[4] The 1966 Yale Milton is also, as we shall see, initially beset with contradictions, from failure to give Milton as polemicist his due.

One can agree with Tillyard[5] and Patrick Cruttwell[6] that he was not a "metaphysical" wit, despite a conceit or two in his earliest English poetry. Nor was he a Restoration wit, though Allan Gilbert[7] found the lustful encounter of Adam and Eve on a "shadie bank" after the Fall suggestive of "the jocose poems" like those in the *Windsor Drollery,* and though misogynistic phrases from *Samson Agonistes* turn up, with lighter weight, in *Aureng-Zebe,* and Etherege and Congreve made similar borrowings.[8] Principally, and because of his principles, Milton lived on in the days of Charles II as an anachronism, but he was strangely updated.

If by any chance the word "wit" is used to hint at a sense of humor, the implication is bound to meet with the most vigorous resistance, for does not everybody know, and has not nearly everybody said, that this was one poet utterly lacking in that important quality? Speak of humor in *Paradise Lost,* and the knowing reader immediately thinks of "No fear lest dinner cool" (V, 396), or Belial's jest, after the infernal cannon have bowled the good angels over, "Leader, the terms we sent were terms of weight, / Of hard contents, and full of force urg'd home, / Such as we might perceive amus'd them all, / And stumbl'd many" (VI, 621–624).

It may be that it takes a devil, today, to be "amused" by these puns. (Accused by Filip von Zesen in 1661 of "teuflischen aberwitz,"[9] Milton had cannonaded Hall in similar fashion: the Remonstrant having spoken of "the battry of their paper-pellets," he was answered: "if pellets will not doe, your owne Canons shall be turn'd against you."[10]) On the other hand, it may be that we are too sadly far from unfallen man to share Adam's innocent "mirth" (IV, 346) on the occasion of the elephant's wreathing "His Lithe Proboscis" (a deliberately ponderous noun that puts the frisky pachyderm before us). Perhaps this is only for children at circuses.

It could be that it is only we who are solemn. For instance, "Our thin decorum is nervous about admitting the comic to proximity with the official sublime."[11] Therefore we fail to appreciate that "No fear lest dinner cool" is "one of the genuinely *achieved* comic lines in English"—fitting into the "domestic, 'middle-class,' comic" that much of the rest of Book V is. The critic who says this is himself funny—"Suppley and brilliantly Milton's picture of Adam and Eve in the garden expands and contracts in a kind of systolic decorum of the needs of the subject"—but all by way of reminder that the angelic digestion is also comic and contains a "dazzling conceit"[12]—pun—: "Your bodies may at last turn all to Spirit, / Improv'd by *tract* of time" (V, 497–498, my italics). As for the so often deplored Book VI, Arnold Stein[13] rescued that by analyzing it as an extended metaphor and intentionally ridiculous.

This is one of the problems. When was Milton smiling? The jest in "At a Vacation Exercise" on a fellow-student named Rivers was lost for two centuries, recovered between the first edition and the second of Volume I of Masson's *Life,* but is still lost to some:[14] for instance, Dora Raymond in 1932[15] complained of "an irrelevant address to the rivers of England"; on the other hand this biographer observed (assisted by Warton), "When asked to indite Latin iambics on the Platonic Idea as Aristotle understood it, this disconcerting student produced such absurdities as to qualify his opus for inclusion in a burlesque book of 1715, made up of specimens of unintelligible metaphysics."[16]

Solemn ourselves, we ought to keep questioning, as Tillyard so often did. Is Sonnet VIII, "Captain or Colonel," "slightly humorous in tone"?[17] Was the poet "making fun of Ellwood when remarking 'pleasantly' that Ellwood had put *Paradise Regained* into his head"?[18] Is the opening of "L'Allegro" a burlesque?[19] Is "or o're the tiles" (*P.L.,* IV, 191) "a perfect touch of deliberate comedy"?[20]

When Milton *is* unmistakeable, we turn aside. "Our" Milton wrote Prolusio VII, on the blessings of knowledge, but not VI, "Sportive Exercises do not stand in the way of Philosophic Studies." Mrs. Tillyard[21] declined to translate some lines of the latter, which make the same unwholesome reference as the ending of Canto XXI of the *Inferno.* (Milton apologized profusely; Dante—Hell was Hell—did not.) The Lady of Christ's was producing the crude humor that was expected. Even the apology was traditional. One old prolusion in manuscript at the University Library, Cambridge[22] begins in English: "Once more welcome as degrees to our inscriptions—in a word you are welcome as you are come. Now why? do not ask me to what, I confess you could not come in a worse time, but such as we have, truly ye have it with a good will. Truly if we had known of your coming and mother had provided something else—but pray set down." Evidently salutatorians have never ceased to struggle, self-consciously, with their obligation to clown.

Most often, Milton's is, admittedly, "grim laughter,"[23] since he lived a life of controversy and used his wit in "Christian warfare." Wit so used is satirical: thus the two key words meet.

Aubrey brought them together long ago: "Extreme pleasant in his conversation, & at dinner, supper &c: but Satyricall. He pronounced the letter R very hard: a certain signe of a Satyricall Witt fr. Jo: Dreyden."[24] In the margin Aubrey added, "Littera canina," for that was what the Roman satirists called the letter R.

"R is the *dog's* letter, and hurrieth in the sound," noted Ben Jonson in his English Grammar.[25] Whatever this meant in the way of a burr,[26] he who was to be the greatest satirist of the age apprehended that it boded not well for those who might stumble across Milton's path. Of course there was hindsight, based on Milton's actual publications, to make such an inference easier. And Dryden may himself have been the victim of a pleasantry when Milton gave him permission to "tag" his lines. Certainly readers of *The State of Innocence and Fall of Man* will be inclined to think so, especially if the blank verse poet went on to say, as one version has it, "some of 'em are so Awkward and Old Fashion'd that I think you had as good leave 'em as you found 'em."[27] It appears that more than one shot was fired in a war between these two about "the jingling sound of like endings," "the troublesome and modern bondage of rhyming," skill in which Dryden considered Milton lacked.[28]

To continue this pairing, is the line in *Mac Flecknoe,* "Thy inoffensive satires never bite" (200) a reminiscence of Joseph Hall's hapless offering of "Toothlesse Satyrs" followed by "byting Satires"?[29] And if so, was Dryden inspired by Milton's merciless logic: "a toothlesse Satyr is as improper as a toothed sleekstone, and as bullish"; "For if it bite neither the persons nor the vices, how is it a Satyr, and if it bite either, how is it toothlesse, so that toothlesse Satyrs are as much as if he had said toothlesse teeth."[30] "Relics of the bum" (*Mac Flecknoe,* 101) echoes a hit in *Defensio Secunda* and *Pro Se Defensio.*[31]

Keeping to English, we can compare a passage from *Of Reformation,* "I know many of those that pretend to be great Rabbies in these studies have scarce saluted them from the strings, and the titlepage, or to give 'em more, have bin but the Ferrets and Moushunts of an Index,"[32] with Pope's "How index-learning turns no student pale, / Yet holds the eel of science by the tail" (*The Dunciad,* I, 280).

Dryden, Pope, even Swift: we can catch Milton and Swift saying the same thing, with the customary 18th-century increase in literalness. Thomas Birch put on record in 1738[33] a bon mot the authenticity of which there seems to be no reason to doubt.

> Mr. [John] *Ward* saw Mrs. [Deborah] *Clarke, Milton's* Daughter, at the House of one of her Relations, not long before her Death, [in 1727] "when she informed me, says that gentleman, that she and her Sisters us'd to read to their Father in eight Languages; which by practice they were capable of doing with great readiness and accuracy, tho' they understood what they read in no other Language but *English;* and their Father us'd often to say in their hearing, *one Tongue was enough for a Woman.*"

It is a reliable line of transmission, from Milton's youngest daughter to Ward, who was professor of rhetoric in Gresham College, to Birch, a diligent gatherer of material who, the very next day after he heard this story from Ward, visited Milton's granddaughter for more information. The jest stuck in Deborah's mind some sixty years, to the end of her life. Her recollection (or Ward's) might be inaccurate on other things: for example, only one of her sisters, not both, shared the task of reading to their father: Phillips, who is more to be trusted here, says that the eldest, Anne, was excused on account of a defect. In short, one can and does forget a bit of life, but not an epigram as coruscating as "One tongue is enough for a woman."

This was or became a proverb.[34] It turns up in Swift's *A Complete Collection of Genteel and Ingenious Conversation,*[35] published the same year as Birch's *Complete Collection,* 1738. Miss Notable at table says, "Pray, Mr. Nerout, will you please to send me a piece of tongue?"—is answered, "Never. By no means, madam: one tongue is enough for a woman."

I make a point of invoking Milton's great successors in the field of devastation because, although one must distinguish between satire as a mode and satire as a form, Dryden, Pope, and Swift are granted licenses that, for three centuries, Milton has been denied. The feeling seems to be that he must not operate on

any level below the grandiose. He often deviated from the sublime and solemn, and most of the time with zest and wit and high
moral purpose, and we miss a great deal by refusing to look and
understand. Not to quote critics who, because of their dates, can
be called old-fashioned, we find the same averted gaze and wring-
ing of hands in the general introduction to Volume IV of the
Yale Prose Works.[36] Here, if anywhere, we should expect appreciation, since it is this volume that gives us, for the first time,
proper annotations to the three *Defences*. We are put on notice
that the accompanying new translations are "distinguished,"[37] but
Milton as a satirist is repeatedly devalued and deplored, though
Mercurius Fumigosus is lavishly quoted and praised,[38] Marcha-
mont Needham approved for writing like Milton[39] (but Milton
ruled out when he writes like Needham), and Sir John Birken-
head identified as "a satirist of remarkable talent and insight."[40]
Let one sentence of the indictment represent the whole: "No
rhetorical device in *A Defence* is more destructive to Milton's
persuasiveness than his persistent use of epithets, the variety and
dullness of which is astonishing in a mind so capacious."[41] I am
able to follow neither the logic nor the grammar. I do not see why
"variety" should be "astonishing in a mind so capacious." I
should think variety would be expected of a capacious mind: and
Milton gives it to us. The use of "is" instead of "are": "the variety
and dullness . . . is astonishing" indicates that for the writer
variety and dullness are close in meaning. Also, the descriptive
"bitter" is applied four times,[42] where I consider it evident that
Milton is enjoying himself hugely, feeling mightily within himself
his resources of learning and argumentation and mockery, as he
takes on, in turn, "the great Kill-cow of *Christendom*" (as Phillips called him[43]), Salmasius, pseudo-Morus, Morus. He was not
being merely personal, at least in the first two *Defences*. As F. E.
Hutchinson[44] has commented, "In some true if incomplete sense
he was delivering to the world, in his first and second *Defence of
the English People,* that epic 'doctrinal and exemplary to a nation,' to which he had early dedicated his powers."

To criticise a polemicist because he has "inflammatory sen-
tences"[45] is comparable to complaining because a sonnet has
fourteen lines or because blank verse does not rhyme. Happily,
the editors or translators of the individual *Defences,* in their
introductions, go their own way. Professor Donald C. Macken-
zie, translator of the first *Defence,* notes, "No one style, in fact,
can handle the variety [here "variety" seems not to be pejorative]
of styles in Milton's Latin. At times it is senatorial rhetoric, and
we hear again Cicero against Catiline or Antony. At times it is
Plautine comedy, earthy in its humor [the general editor had said
it was "unrelieved even by humor or lightness"[46]] and delighting in
puns. "At times the dominant tone is the satirist's *saeva indigna-
tio.*"[47] Professor Donald A. Roberts calls attention to "the varied
play of wit, and the rhetorical brilliance of *Defensio Secunda*"
and identifies its form, "panegyric and diatribe."[48]

The following passage from Lillian Feder's article, "John Dryden's Use of Classical Rhetoric,"[49] fits Milton so well that we
could substitute his name throughout:

> Dryden here [*A Defence of an Essay of Dramatic Poesy*]
> combines the image of the warrior in the chivalric trial by
> combat with that of the orator engaged in a verbal battle.
> There are interesting parallels in the writings of Cicero and
> Quintilian, both of whom frequently use the image of a
> battle or a gladitorial contest when referring to an argu-
> ment in the law court or forum. Often in an extended
> image, combining the language of oratory with that of phys-
> ical combat, they picture the orator debating *in aciem
> forensam.* In the same way, Dryden depicts himself as
> the orator at arms. His cause is a good one, and, like a good
> orator, he must find the right arguments and their proper
> arrangement. Indeed, this is no mere literary dispute; it is an
> argument that will bring *honor* and *glory* to the winner. So
> significant is the contest that Dryden uses as an image the
> hereditary champion of England.

What was Edward Phillips' language about the combat with Salmasius: "there could no where have been found a Champion that durst lift up the Pen against so formidable an Adversary, had not our little *English David* had the Courage to undertake this great *French Goliah,* to whom he gave such a hit in the Forehead, that he presently staggered, and soon after fell."[50] We are not dealing with a "cloister'd vertue, . . . that never sallies out and sees her adversary."[51] The Bohn edition misprinted, "seeks her adversary," and many eminent scholars and critics have so quoted *Areopagitica,* and ultimately they are right, for a closely parallel passage in *Pro Se Defensio* has "hostem petere."[52]

J. Milton French's theory was that Milton was divided, that he suffered a dichotomy between the poet in him and the rationalist, that, indeed, his "mind . . . was essentially critical rather than creative."[53] I find this easier to believe of A. E. Housman, who wrote tender lyrics, while mercilessly pillorying other scholars in his classical prefaces and reviews. It should not be possible to forget how much of Milton's poetry takes the form of debate and symbolic combat: The Lady versus Comus, the forces of good in *Paradise Lost* versus the forces of evil, Samson versus Dalila and Harapha, Jesus versus the Tempter. (Has there been any complaint that Jesus, with whom Milton probably identifies as much as with Samson, is curt rather than courteous to his opponent?) Lines 108–131 of "Lycidas" constitute the author's first antiprelatical tract. How far back can we go in this lifelong pattern, leaving out the scholastic exercises? "L'Allegro" versus "Il Penseroso"?

It is just possible that Milton made his debut as a polemicist with his "Paraphrase on *Psalm* 114," "done . . . at fifteen years old." One wonders why, of the 150 psalms, it was No. 114 that was chosen. (Given 114, 136 will follow, for its similar theme.) True, it characteristically, prophetically, gratifyingly, sounds the note of "liberty." But, in 1623, liberty from whom, from what? King James? Archbishop Abbot, who was in virtual retirement because he had killed a keeper in a hunting accident and who in any case was believed to be in sympathy with the Puritans? The clue may lie in a letter of John Chamberlain's[54] about the rejoicing of the people of London, in October, 1623, when Prince Charles returned from Spain without the Infanta, whom it was feared he would bring back as his Roman Catholic bride. There were bonfires in the streets, and "A number of other particulers I could set downe too long to relate, but among all there beeing solemne service in Powles the singing of a new antheme was specially observed, the 114th psalme, when Israell came out of Egipt and the house of Jacob from among the barbarous people." Thus, from the St. Paul's schoolboy, we could be getting something of a political allegory, like *Absalom and Achitophel,* with "Israel" meaning England in both heroic-couplet poems.

An analytical survey needs to be made of Milton's puns.[55] How many reverberations has "hollow states" in the sonnet to Vane (cf. "hollow truce," *P.L.,* VI, 578)? When Camus comes "footing slow" ("Lycidas," 103), does "footing" subliminally conceal the word *pedant?*[56] Certainly this scholar is an inveterate etymologist and lexicographer, which is the apologia for "Ravens . . . Though ravenous" (*P.R.,* II, 269). In *Areopagitica* he uses "enchiridion"[57] to mean a manual of devotion, but cannot forget that it also signifies a dagger. In the same work, "our London trading *St. Thomas* in his vestry"[58] is multilevelled: 1. Trading was going on within supposedly "hallowed limits" in Cheapside. 2. It was trading in clothing: thus "vestry" is a pun. 3. The pun is strengthened by the recollection that "St. Thomas" was the older name of the Mercers' chapel (and *mercenary* is latent here: Milton launched all this with reference to the vending of sermons). 4. St. Thomas received the Virgin Mary's girdle on her Assumption. 5. Milton has been attacking the vestments of the clergy since *Of Reformation.* In stride now, we next get, "and adde to boot St. *Martin,* and St. *"Hugh,"* which conveys us by way of the saint who shared his cloak (and the liberty of St. Martin le Grand, where petty commerce was as rife as under the

nave of St. Paul's) to the unofficial patron saint of shoemakers—
from vestments to boots, sheer fun-making: there was no church
dedicated to St. Hugh in London.

In Latin controversy his exuberance in this kind knows no
bounds. Bitter? It is hilarious. The syca*more* complex of puns is
one of the most ingenious ever erected.[59] (But Milton began
sporting with "moratus sum"—"I have delayed" and "I have
played the fool": to combine both meanings, a translator would
have to resort to, "I've fooled around enough"—at the end of
Prolusio VI,[60] a word-play that dates back to Nero, as there
noted.) Where can we find a more stunning retort—literally a
twisting back—than the transmutation of More's gibe, "Orestis
aemule" ("O emulous of Orestes!"—i.e. madman) to "O restis
aemule" ("O emulous of a rope!")?[61] Give a fool a little
room—and he'll hang himself.

The nickname of the maid of Salmasius is altered from "Bon-
tia" to "Pontia," because it is more fruitful that way, yielding
Latin *pons,* "bridge," Greek *pontus,* "sea," pontifex, Pontius
Pilate, Pontia—a woman who poisoned her children, and the
region of Pontus, with its various demeaning legends. To look at
a clause of multiple reference that still needs annotation, More is
accused: "qui denique totam illam Pontiae Sestiada sicco pede
praeterieris"[62]: "you who, in fine, would pass over, with dry foot,
that whole Sestiad of Pontia." In other words, More is trying to
skip over an amorous scandal involving himself and Pontia. He is
not good at *praeteritio*—that is, he is as wretched a rhetorician as
he is a man. "Sestiada," a Greek accusative singular of a word
that dates back to Musaeus, is an allusion to the Marlowe-
Chapman poem *Hero and Leander,*[63] which is in "sestiads," a
term Chapman used to refer both to Sestos, Hero's home in
Thrace, and to the six parts into which he divided the poem. We
have "Alexander the Phrygian" (Paris, the great lover) More
crossing the Helles*pont* (was it Hell for him, after Pontia dug
her nails into his face?) without getting his feet wet. (Xerxes
did accomplish that, by means of pontoons.) The implication is

that he would make a fitting subject for a mock epic. (Does he think he is a divinity that he can go dry-footed like Circe: "Summaque decurrit pedibus super aequora siccis"—Ovid's *Metamorphoses*, XIV, 50.) It is ridiculous, and it is as pointless to feel sorry for him as for Shadwell, but where Dryden wrote a lampoon, Milton is still out to correct and reform: besides defending himself, he is a spokesman for a side that he believes to be right.

Let us give up the old pastime of opposing Milton's left hand to his right, when the complicated truth is that he was ambidextrous, his *ingenium* a two-handed engine serving poetry and reform.

State University of New York at Albany

NOTES

1. It has been a generation since J. Milton French's pioneering article, "Milton as Satirist," *PMLA*, LI (1936), 414–29.

2. *The Reason of Church-Government Urg'd against Prelaty*, Columbia Milton (hereafter abbreviated as CM), III, 232.

3. "Milton in Rustication," *SP*, XIX (1922), 116.

4. Isabel Gamble MacCaffrey, editor, Milton's *"Samson Agonistes" and the Shorter Poems* (New York, 1966), pp. ix, xv, xxiv.

5. *The Metaphysicals and Milton* (London, 1956), pp. 61–74.

6. *The Shakespearean Moment* (New York, 1960), pp. 203 ff.

7. *SAMLA Studies in Milton*, ed. J. Max Patrick (Gainesville, 1953), "Milton's Defense of Bawdry," pp. 65 f.

8. E. S. Le Comte, *"Samson Agonistes* and *Aureng-Zebe,"* *Etudes Anglaises*, XI (1958), 18–22; Martin A. Larson, "The Influence of Milton's Divorce Tracts on Farquhar's *Beaux Stratagem,"* *PMLA*, XXXIX (1924), 174–78; in Act II of *The Way of the World* Millamant's entrance is a take-off on Dalila's (*S.A.*, 710 ff.): "Here she comes, i' faith, full sail, with her fan spread and her streamers out, and a shoal of fools for tenders."

9. William Riley Parker, *Milton's Contemporary Reputation* (Columbus, 1940), p. 107. French, *Life Records of John Milton*, IV (New

Brunswick, 1956), 358, translates "aberwitz" as "craziness"; it is, rather, "false strained wit."

10. *Animadversions,* CM, III, 143.

11. Thomas Kranidas, "Adam and Eve in the Garden: A study of *Paradise Lost,* Book V," *SEL,* IV (1964), 71.

12. *Ibid.,* pp. 78, 72, 82–83, 81. This article is very different from Gregory Ziegelmaier's "The Comedy of *Paradise Lost," College English,* XXVI (1965), 516–22, which, dwelling on the "Cosmic Laughter" or "Divine Humor," is depressingly reminiscent of Dr. Johnson's famous review of Soame Jenyns' *Free Enquiry into the Nature and Origin of Evil* (in Johnson's *Works,* Oxford, 1825, VI, 47 ff.).

13. *Answerable Style* (Minneapolis, 1953), pp. 17–37.

14. What is undoubtedly the most widely used college text, Merritt Y. Hughes' edition of the *Complete Poems and Major Prose* (New York, 1957), has dropped the note to line 91 that was in the same editor's *"Paradise Regained," The Minor Poems, and "Samson Agonistes"* (New York, 1937), p. 116.

15. *Oliver's Secretary* (New York), p. 15.

16. *Ibid.,* p. 12.

17. *Milton* (New York, 1930), p. 138. G. M. Trevelyan called it "a jesting sonnet" (*England under the Stuarts,* London, 1947, p. 197).

18. *Milton,* p. 299.

19. *The Miltonic Setting* (London, 1938), pp. 1–28.

20. *Studies in Milton* (New York, 1951), p. 74.

21. Milton, *Private Correspondence and Academic Exercises,* trans. Phyllis B. Tillyard (Cambridge, 1932), p. 94. She also does not locate the lice, p. 97: cf. CM, XII, 236.

22. Dd. 6. 30. P. 22v.

23. *Animadversions,* CM, III, 107.

24. Helen Darbishire, editor, *The Early Lives of Milton* (London, 1932), p. 6.

25. *Works,* ed. William Gifford (Boston, 1853), p. 899.

26. Probably the idiosyncrasy was most noticeable with preconsonantal r, which in London was on its modern way out; Milton was again being old-fashioned. Cf. Helge Kökeritz, *Shakespeare's Pronunciation* (New Haven, 1953), p. 315.

27. Darbishire, p. 335.

28. David Masson, *Life of John Milton,* VI (London, 1880), 633 ff.; Morris Freedman, "Milton and Dryden on Rhyme," *HLQ,* XXIV (1961), 337–44.

29. Dryden's *Poetical Works,* ed. George R. Noyes (Boston, 1950), p. 1060.

30. *Animadversions,* CM, III, 114; *An Apology,* CM, III, 329.

31. CM, VIII, 176; IX, 172.

32. CM, III, 35.

33. Editor, *A Complete Collection of the Historical, Political, and Miscellaneous Works of John Milton* (London), I, lxi-ii.

34. Morris Palmer Tilley, *A Dictionary of the Proverbs in England in the Sixteenth and Seventeenth Centuries* (Ann Arbor, 1950), p. 675 (T 398).

35. In *A Tale of a Tub, the Battle of the Books, and other Satires,* (Everyman's Library), p. 299.

36. Ed. Don M. Wolfe (New Haven, 1966).

37. *Ibid.,* pp. 102, 109 (footnotes).

38. *Ibid.,* pp. 203 ff.

39. *Ibid.,* pp. 49 ff., 124.

40. *Ibid.,* p. 207.

41. *Ibid.,* p. 114.

42. *Ibid.,* pp. 109, 231, 252, 257.

43. Darbishire, p. 70.

44. *Milton and the English Mind* (New York, 1948), p. 84. Cf. Tillyard, *Milton,* p. 198, and Sir H. J. C. Grierson, *Milton and Wordsworth* (Cambridge, 1937), pp. 71–72.

45. Yale Milton IV, 91.

46. *Ibid.,* p. 112.

47. *Ibid.,* p. 296.

48. *Ibid.,* pp. 538, 540.

49. *PMLA,* LXIX (1954), p. 1262 (see footnote 9 there for full references).

50. Darbishire, p. 70.

51. CM, IV, 311.

52. CM, IX, 224. Further discussion in my *Milton Dictionary* (New York, 1961), s.v. "Bohn edition"; *Yet Once More: Verbal and Psychological Pattern in Milton* (New York, 1953), p. 149. Besides following in the classical tradition of adversary oratory, Milton is in the line of the flytings of the humanists. Charles Nisard's *Les Gladiateurs de la République des Lettres aux XVe, XVIe et XVIIe Siécles* (Paris, 1860), which does not mention him, illustrates his techniques in detail. Since a recent critic has defended George Herbert's pattern poems on the ground that he was not the first to do them, it may be comforting to know that Milton was not the

first to call an opponent a "Pork" (*Colasterion,* CM, IV, 250): Poggio had called Filelfo that (Nisard, p. 127). Whatever we think of the answer "Ha, ha, ha" (*Animadversions,* CM, III, 170), it is not peculiar to Milton: it can be found before him (*The Marprelate Tracts,* ed. William Pierce, London, 1911, p. 32) and after him (*The Man in the Moon,* quoted—without this connection—in Yale Milton IV, 18). Sir Thomas More's name had been made free with, by his enemies as well as by his friends, a point with which Alexander More consoled himself early in his *Fides Publica.*

53. "Milton as a Historian," *PMLA,* L (1935), 476.

54. *Letters,* ed. Norman E. McClure (Philadelphia, 1939), II, 516.

55. I do not mean that the subject has not often been touched on, usually in deprecation. There are some quotations from commentators, a brief bibliography, and acute original comments in the "Word-Play" section of *Milton's Grand Style* by Christopher Ricks (Oxford, 1963), pp. 66–75; cf. 15. James Brown reaps much from "Fruitless embraces" (*P.L.,* V, 215), pp. 16–17 and 25 of "Eight Types of Puns," *PMLA,* LXXI (1956).

56. J. Mitchell More, "A Pun in 'Lycidas,' " *N & Q,* n.s. V (1958), 211.

57. CM, IV, 329.

58. *Ibid.,* p. 335.

59. *Defensio Secunda,* CM, VIII, 32.

60. CM, XII, 246.

61. CM treats this spacing as a typographical error: IX, 304. Let us hope not, even though there is an undoubted slip (of the same kind) two words before. Puns are aural: Milton was in his element, alert for the kill.

62. *Pro Se Defensio,* CM, IX, 188.

63. It is first an allusion to Musaeus' *Hero and Leander,* but that Milton has English literature on his mind is shown by his reference in the next clause to *Romeo and Juliet,* for so I take "Tibaltianam"—in a context of love and quarreling—to be. Records have been searched in vain for a girl of that name.

JERUSALEM AND ATHENS: THE TEMPTATION OF LEARNING IN "PARADISE REGAINED"

B. Rajan

When the devil offers Dr. Faustus the riches of infinite knowledge all of us (including Marlowe, according to recent critics) disapprove of the doctor's choice. When Christ in *Paradise Regained* rejects a similar offer from a more insidious antagonist he is greeted with anguished cries of *et tu Brute!* Donne can describe a "hydroptique immoderate desire of learning" as the "worst voluptuousness"[1]: but more moderate language in Milton's brief epic is generally found to be far less tolerable. These remarks are not made to subscribe to the familiar lament that critics are inconsistent but rather to suggest that there is a problem of how to respond involved here which is more than the problem of what Christ says or even of how he says it. For this reason the search for precedents is only of limited usefulness. To prefer Jerusalem to Athens is not solely a late Puritan or a patristic privilege. Sidney can be quoted to the same effect and so can Nicholas Ferrar.[2] Plotinus's concept of the virtues as purifications and his specific definition of magnanimity as the scorn of earthly things can also be made to point in the same direction.[3] On the other side, Luther and Calvin can be quoted on the benefits of literature.[4] This exchange of accepted positions can serve to remind us that the circulation of ideas is rather more complex than it appears to be in the first stage of scholarship. It also becomes apparent that it is not in this way that we can discover why Milton did what he did.

Douglas Bush's concern at watching Milton "turn and rend some main roote of his being"[5] is eloquently put and widely shared. The other side of this observation is hardly ever mentioned. It is that the position which Christ articulates has itself a main root in Milton's being.[6] The much-quoted digression in *The Reason of Church Government*[7] suggests strongly the superiority of the Bible to secular accomplishment not simply as wisdom but as literature. Certain contrary pulls or to continue with the previous metaphor, certain entanglements in the main roots are necessary if the whole mind is to preserve its wholeness. As time passes and a man's sense of the truth as he finds it alters, it is natural that one element or another in these conflicts should predominate. *Paradise Regained* presumably disturbs us because what is taking place in it seems to be more than a mere change of emphasis; crucial attachments which we are accustomed to call Miltonic are being not so much minimized as driven out of existence. Critics aware of these obliterations have suggested that Christ turns his back on history because history chose to turn its back on Milton and that it is the failure of the millenium to materialize which leads to the proclamation of the paradise within. These justifications from life, or from literary life are reassuring only up to a point. A man may be constrained to say certain things but that does not mean that his saying them is aesthetic. The force of rejection is a powerful component in any mind that is God-oriented but there is no obligation to construct a poem which is designed primarily as a demonstration of this force. It is the consistency of the undertaking which deters us. Renunciations, including even this one, are acceptable as gestures or even commitments but not as commitments of the whole man. They disturb us when they are fitted into a process of refusal which drives both the poem and the reader against the wall.

One of the results of a historical examination is that it shows us how unnecessary the wall is. There is no temptation of learning in the Bible and Elizabeth Pope in her pioneering study of the traditions behind *Paradise Regained*[8] has been unable to point to any tradition which sanctions such a temptation. Poets of course, are free to invent what the past fails to offer them; but unless a poet is obstinately obtuse he does not box himself in a situation from which he is unable to escape, at least to his own satisfaction. The question which Satan asks may allow only one right answer. But why, precisely, does the question have to be asked? This is perhaps the most teasing of a number of Miltonic perplexities, including the battle in heaven, Michael's postscript in the last book of *Paradise Lost* and the confrontation between Comus and the Lady.

Despite its provocativeness, the temptation of Athens has received relatively cursory treatment in studies of *Paradise Regained*. The fullest scrutiny of it so far is by Barbara Lewalski[9] and even Mrs. Lewalski in her zealous examination of the genre, can find only one other brief epic on Christ's temptation.[10] A temptation similar to the temptation of Athens apparently occurs in Quarles's *Job Militant*.[11] This is an interesting but scarcely substantial precedent. For the rest, Mrs. Lewalski tells us that epics both brief and compendious, include episodes on the education of the hero.[12] This is a fragile basis for the confident assertion that the need for a temptation of Athens was, so to speak, found by Milton among his *données*.[13] An education involving the rejection of education is a striking reversal of not very compelling precedents. When the reversal is placed in its setting it may well strike us as characteristically Miltonic, but to make it less (or more) than an obsession with renunciation we need to locate it in a larger movement of irony.

Originality invites but seldom receives evaluation on its own terms and that is why, at this point in the poem, arguments from

the genre, the lines and the life will not suffice. There is a driving
internal logic to the poem. We have to possess it, or at least to
recognize it, before we can understand how the force of that logic
annexes precedent or disregards it in the momentum of its unfolding.

Loyalty to its own dramatic decorum can be decisive in shaping the way in which a poem reveals itself. That Christ ought to
be Christ rather than John Milton is a proposition which few
would want to dispute but it is unfortunately not naive to ask
how this proposition operates in the indispositions of *Paradise
Regained* and in the specific tactics of what Louis Martz terms
the "meditative combat."[14] One of the more important among
Professor Pope's recoveries of tradition is her insistence that
Christ suffered the temptations in his human aspect.[15] This fact
like the dialogue in heaven in *Paradise Lost,* provides a dramatic
"cover" for Milton's theology; but it also means that Christ enters
the combat with a crucial unawareness of himself. Both the
achieving of identity and the rejection of those masks which offer
a superficial at the expense of a radical function are caught in
counter-movements, exactly opposed and balanced. Every retreat
from Satan is an advance into self-realization and on a more
spacious stage, every abstention from history helps to create even
in its apparent withdrawal the only basis on which history can be
transformed. It is for this reason that the emphasis in Milton's
brief epic falls so heavily on the second and central temptation.[16] Readers familiar with Milton will recognize a typical
strategy: the redistribution of formal weights so as to reveal the
direction and energy of the main thrust.[17] The inner kingdom
must be constituted with almost vehement purity if the world of
creative action (as distinct from mere turbulence) is to come into
being around it. The perfect man can only become himself
through an unqualified fidelity to the commitments which create
him.

To know these facts the reader of the poem does not have to be
a seventeenth century reader though he cannot but profit from

the attempt to pass imaginatively through the seventeenth century response. What is essential is that the reader should encircle the poem with some general knowledge of Christ's function and his destiny, watching the circle shrink as Christ's realization of himself advances. Then, in the climax on the pinnacle, it will be Christ's knowledge which surprises the reader's knowledge.

Accidents are rare in Milton's poetry and it is no accident that three temptations (or inquiries) in the abstract precede the specific offer of the kingdoms of the world. "Riches" and "Fortune" are suggested first, then "glory" and finally "zeal and duty." The movement is from the material to the apparently "moral," from personal fullfillment to public service. Christ's answers progressively declare his nature: the emphasis on sovereignty in the kingdom of the self needs to be followed if it is to be saved from egotism, by the conviction that glory is found only in serving the glory of God and finally by the realization that even fitness for action must wait on the ripeness of things. The sequence shows Satan's imprisonment in his own earlier manifesto—"Honour, dominion, glory and renown"[18]—and also suggests the nature of what may be called Christ's vertical allegiance in contrast to Satan's horizontal involvement in the world.

It is only after Christ has demonstrated what we may doubly call his uprightness that Satan transports him to that hilltop from which he views history and is exhorted to enter it. The first Adam also saw history from a hilltop and *Paradise Lost* XI, 381–84 carefully makes the link; but the link supports dramatic differences. The first Adam looks on a river of destruction which flows from his sin and which he is powerless to modify. The second, offered the means of decisive involvement, remains the detached and seemingly indifferent observer. Christ's answer has the clarity of Michael's in *Paradise Lost* XII, 82–101 and clarity of certain kinds must skirt the edge of cruelty. But Christ does also add with a confidence increasingly threatening to Satan, that what will be will be irresistibly in its due time. The poem as elsewhere has its tact at these points, its carefully limited bounda-

ries which it asks the reader to cross, bringing his own knowledge
into the poem so that he can measure Satan's blindness and
Christ's advance into self-realization. What happens in the poem
is never the poem's whole story. The stingingly harsh judgment
on Rome for example

> What wise and valiant man could hope to free
> These thus degenerate by themselves enslaved
> Or could of inward slaves make outward free? (IV, 143–45)

work in many ways on the reader's responsiveness. The words
"wise and valiant" are meant to recall our first glimpse of the first
Adam in Paradise (IV, 297). The coupling between interior and
exterior freedom embodies a conviction that Milton states in
many places and in many ways but always with a persistent
fervour of commitment. The controlled play of the sibilants is
also remarkable, curling as it were, in the air of the speaker's
scorn. But most important of all, the reader should be aware that
Christ *is* that second Adam, that wise and valiant man who is
destined to rescue mankind from slavery. The knowledge under-
cuts the otherwise patrician hauteur of the statement and helps us
to realize that Christ in rejecting one kingship is establishing
another. Limited interventions are no substitute for radical trans-
formation. This is surely the purport of the images of kingship in
IV, 146–51.[19] Too little and too late is not part of the strategy of
the divine will. There is no reason why Satan should be advised
of these facts but the reader errs in adopting Satan's blindness.

The division between the second and third books of *Paradise
Regained* cuts perplexingly across the temptation of the kingdoms. One result is to bring Rome and Athens together, thus
giving additional weight to the rejection of the classical world
and compounding Milton's "betrayal" of himself. Another consequence is to arouse a sense of uncertainty regarding the unfolding
of the poem, since a new book can scarcely begin where a crucial
temptation is traditionally supposed to end. Satan himself (IV,
85–90) suggests strongly that after Rome he has no more king-

doms to offer and when Rome is rejected he can do no more than offer again with additional conditions, something that has already been rejected. This is a nice touch of dramatic verisimilitude, bringing us firmly to the end of the temptation in Luke and also suggesting the exasperation of an outwitted opponent who has made his last throw. The second round is over and yet there are indications that it may only be beginning. Other readers besides those in the seventeenth century can draw the conclusion that the devil is most dangerous when he appears to be defeated.

If we look back on IV, 88–9 we will note that Satan says only that he has shown Christ all the kingdoms of the world. Of course there is a kingdom not of this world. Christ has been saying so throughout the poem, sometimes to the extent of appearing to say nothing else. What can be more artful than to offer him that which has hitherto made him invulnerable, to seduce him with those riches in the name of which he has refused all other riches? Seen in this light the temptation of Athens has little to do with Milton's "disillusionment," with his zeal for precedent or his passion for innovation. It is a move issuing strictly out of the logic of combat. In the nature of things it cannot be the *coup de grace* but reserved applause should not be out of order.

Satan's offer is necessarily tainted. Being a citizen of the world (the use of the phrase reminds us how to measure it) he has offered both Parthia and Rome as prizes of the lower glory. Now, in prefacing his most insidious temptation with the words "Be famous" and in his betraying reference to "empire" (a categorical imperative of the Satanic mind) he forgets Christ's calm dismissal of these lures in III, 44–47. More important, as a citizen of the world, he can only offer that wisdom which the world has accumulated in its history. He cannot know that there is a higher wisdom; but the reader should know it and Christ should not only know it but should remind us through the shaping of his answer that he is destined to incarnate that wisdom.

The preamble to Satan's temptation is hardly ever quoted. It is among the most crucial passages in *Paradise Regained* and it is essential that we grasp its implications firmly if we are to know what is happening in the poem.

> All knowledge is not couched in Moses' Law,
> The Pentateuch or what the Prophets wrote;
> The Gentiles also know, and write, and teach
> To admiration, led by Nature's light: (IV, 225–28).

What is being offered is the completion of the world of understanding, with natural knowledge supplementing the wisdom of the law and of the prophets. Christ can agree with the first two lines of the statement; but he cannot agree with the consequence since he himself is to bring Old Testament wisdom to a far more decisive and transforming fulfillment. Satan offers all that he can within the limits of his knowing but Christ at this point in his "becoming," not only knows but *is* something that Satan cannot understand. A deep irony turns here on the reader's recognition of what is going on. Christ *must* refuse Athens to declare his nature not necessarily in his capacity as perfect man but rather in his capacity as the historic Christ who is to bring down into history a power of grace beyond the light of nature.[20] His reference to the inner light, received from the fountain of light is not, as critics tend to suggest, a walling-up of himself in the interior kingdom. Rather it is a statement of the additional dimension that is to be bestowed upon the kingdoms of the world. It is also an oblique affirmation to Satan that Christ is truly the Son of God, deriving all that he knows and is from that allegiance. Satan's difficulties with the concept of sonship are recurrent and characteristic but once again the reader is not called on to adopt his exclusions.

"Error by his own aims is best evinced"[21] is the devil's invitation to engage in the wars of truth. Christ's answer can only be that error is trapped in its own being and is best shown to be error by virtue of a source outside itself. If the light of nature is to be redeemed by the light of grace, if the law is to culminate in the gospel, he who brings the higher wisdom into history can scarcely

accept the lower as a substitute. It is indeed the higher understanding which gives structure and cohesion to that lesser knowledge, which is not really knowledge but vanity, until what is
above it puts it into order. Christ who commands the power of
creative ordering (as he did in the seventh book of *Paradise
Lost*) can scarcely surrender that power to the very substance
which it is supposed to transform.

Comus has his fling at Stoicism's "budge doctors" and Stoic
apathy is on the agenda of the philosophic angels in hell.[22] Christ
attacks Stoicism with a distinctive earnestness which is only un-
derstandable when we think of him as himself rather than as an
articulation of Milton's disappointments. Christ has defended the
interior kingdom and is now being offered that kingdom precisely
because of the consistency of his defence. Stoicism is the affirmation of that kingdom as an end rather than as an instrument for
the service of God's glory. Noble in its indifference to the world,
it is potentially Satanic in its self-centredness: this is the cutting
edge of Christ's reference to "pride" a reference that is not
without dramatic pointedness when we remember to whom
Christ is replying. Christ's dismissal of the schools has a finality
for which "frigid" is almost certainly the wrong adjective. We are
facing the decisiveness of a man who has come to judge the world
rather than to receive it, or rather to receive it and to redeem it as
its judge. The strangely neglected lines which follow make abun-
dantly clear where we ought to be in our own minds.

> Alas what can they teach, and not mislead
> Ignorant of themselves, of God much more,
> And how the world began, and how man fell,
> Degraded by himself, on grace depending? (IV, 309–12)

It is the accents of compassion rather than scorn which are
dominant. Regardless of the injunction of the Delphic oracle,
man cannot know himself until he finds within himself the
primeval act by which he was undone. Philosophies which evade
this fact have set themselves upon the road to delusion. The

second line of the statement is carefully ambiguous. If we are ignorant of our limited selves we must be far more ignorant of God who is unlimited. But our ignorance of ourselves is also the result of our not knowing God and so the greater ignorance, in the movement of the thought, reflects back on the lesser and inexorably enlarges it. As for the beginning of the world, Satan has reason to remember that; it was the response of divine creativeness to the damage done by his own rebellion. The fall of man is also an event of which Satan is keenly and perhaps delectably aware. A common knowledge denied to Athens is thus being assumed between the combatants and it might almost seem at this stage in the response, as if Christ were reminding Satan as a privileged individual "in the know," of the philosophic delusions of the Gentiles. Yet the very next phrase "Degraded by himself," is a stab at Satan's vanity and "on grace depending" carries us into a realm with which Christ's opponent is totally unfamiliar. The reader must remember the stern distinction of *Paradise Lost,* III, 129–32, a distinction which was well-known outside the epic. Even more important than the drawing of the boundaries of Satan's world is our sense of the point that Christ has reached in the affirmation and becoming of himself. For the first time, he knows himself as the instrument of grace, implicitly answering and softening the question which he had implacably posed in rejecting the temptation of Rome. He also makes clear what he must do with Athens. The light of nature though "not in all quite lost"[23] has been drastically dimmed by man's fall. Christ's task is to restore that light and not to use it. Satan cannot know of Christ's redemptive mission (an ignorance which gives depth to the angry bewilderment of IV, 368–72) but the reader ought to know and is now put on notice of what he ought to know. Seen in this frame of understanding, Christ's remarks all fall into a firmly shaped perspective. His historic function is not to live in Athens but to make what is of value in Athens live in him.

The context of the *genre* and of interpretative tradition are thus not quite sufficient for the reading of *Paradise Regained.*

There is a dramatic encirclement which irradiates the poem and which is drawn into the poem by the poem's shaping forces. As the duel of the mind evolves in its stripped clarity we are meant to measure each movement of the combatants with an intentness not inferior to that of the writing itself. Irony is the word which seems to be called for however much the term may have been debased by usage: both the irony of Christ's increasing self-embodiment, abutted against Satan's static yet sedulous resourcefulness and the irony of the reader's larger knowledge, measuring both the growing and the imprisoned identity. When Christ's words are interpreted according to the logic of combat and according to the destiny he is to take on and increasingly knows, they cease to be intrusions of the poet into the poem and become aesthetic facts rather than aesthetic disturbances. Not all problems of imaginative acceptance disappear, since the basic commitment set forth with typical severity, is well beyond our powers of adherence and also involves the disconcerting paradox of using literature for the denial of literature. But a properly constructed dramatic whole calls for contemplation of its forces rather than endorsement of its doctrine. Moreover, every rejection in the poem is meant to be subverted by the reader's realization that it is only through the quality of his refusals that Christ is able to construct that historic personality which is destined eventually to redeem what is rejected.[24]

The question of what can be legitimately read into a poem will always remain debatable and provocative. There are many poems which in the course of their tactics, invite the reader to write part of them himself; the act of reading thus becomes a specific foundation for growth in the reader's own mind. Any student of rhetoric also knows that the most effective persuasions are better left unsaid. This kind of poetic tact is not always easy to separate from incompetence but in *Paradise Regained* the evidence is all on the side of a tact that is finely controlled and purposive, drawing its boundaries with precise insinuation so that we are persuaded across them into a surrounding and creative irony. There is yet another kind of "extension" of a poem for which we must be prepared to allow. As the reading situation changes and traditions drop away, connections which were once "live" cease to exist and crucial lights in the poem may no longer shine as the reader reads. Historical scholarship can switch on these lights; its temptation is perhaps to switch on too many of them and so to minimize the poem's powers of self-illumination even in the darkness of today. *Paradise Regained* is a poem difficult of access but when one has become familiar with the special kind of alertness that it calls for, it is remarkable to what an extent it is capable of sustaining and validating itself. Rich associations that once invested it can and should be drawn back into it; but a reading educated in vigilance and freed from unaesthetic distractions, can still perceive much that remains on the poem's own grounds.

University of Western Ontario

NOTES

1. Donne also maintains that "David is a better poet than Virgil" (*The Sermons of John Donne,* ed. Simpson and Porter, Berkeley 1953–62, Vol. IV, p. 167).

2. In the *Defence of Poesy* Sidney observes: "Nay truly learned men have learnedly thought, that where once reason has so much over-mastered passion as that the mind has a free desire to do well, the inward light each mind has in itself is as good as a philosopher's book." The similarity to Christ's argument in *P.R.* need not be laboured. Ferrar in *Ferrar Papers,* p. 63, is more emphatic: "In as much as all the Comedyes, Tragedyes, Pastoralls &c: & all those they call Heroicall Poems, none excepted; & like wise all the Bookes of Tales, wᶜʰ they call Novells, & all feigned Historyes written in Prose, all love Hymns, & all the like Bookes are full of Idolatry, & especially tend to the Overthrow of Christian Religion, undermining the very Foundations thereof, & corrupt & pollute the minds of the Readers, with filthy lusts, as, woe is me,

I have proved in my self. In this regard, therefore, to show my detestation of them to the World, & that others may take warning, I have burned all of them, & most humbly have, & do beseech God, to forgive me all my mispent time in them, & all the Sinns that they have caused in me, wch surely, but for his infinite Grace, had carryed my soule down into Hell long ere this."

3. *Enneads* 1, 6, 6.

4. In *Institutes* 2.2.16 Calvin observes: "If the Lord has willed that we be helped in physics, dialectic, mathematics, and other like disciplines, by the work and ministry of the ungodly let us use this assistance." Luther declares that those who consider a knowledge of scripture alone apart from the classics as sufficient "must always remain irrational brutes": *Luther on Education* (St. Louis, n.d.) p. 183. The thing said changes according to the polemical context and Luther can be quoted differently as in Barbara Lewalski, *Milton's Brief Epic* (London, 1966), pp. 295–96. Augustine in *De Doctrina Christiana* (Bk. 11, Chapter 40) tells us that "the beliefs of the Gentiles contain not only fables and invented superstitions and useless requirements of labour, which each of us must despise and shun as we follow Christ out of the pagan world, but also the liberal arts, which are more proper for the use of truth, and certain precepts useful in governing our lives, even verities which reveal the one God."

5. *The Renaissance and English Humanism* (Toronto, 1939), p. 125. For kindred observations by others see B. K. Lewalski, *op. cit.*, p. 282.

6. The argument is advanced more emphatically in Bush's *John Milton* (London, 1965), pp. 189 ff and in his edition of Milton's poetry (New York, 1965), p. 461. See also Irene Samuel, "Milton on Learning and Wisdom," *PMLA*, LXIV (1949), pp. 708–23.

7. *Yale* 1, pp. 808–23. The view (p. 816) that "those frequent songs throughout the law and prophets . . . not in their divine argument alone, but in the very critical art of composition may be easily made appear over all the kinds of lyrick poesy to be incomparable" is specifically remembered in *P.R.* IV 334–49.

8. *Paradise Regained: the Tradition and the Poem* (reissued New York; 1962).

9. B. K. Lewalski, *op. cit.*, pp. 281–302. Mention must also be made of Arnold Stein's thoughtful comments in *Heroic Knowledge* (Minneapolis, 1957), pp. 94–111.

10. Lewalski, *op. cit.*, p. 66.

11. *Ibid.*, p. 120.

12. *Ibid.*, p. 128.

13. *Ibid.,* p. 127.

14. *"Paradise Regained:* the Meditative Combat," *ELH,* XXVII (1960), pp. 223–47.

15. Pope, *op. cit.,* pp. 13–29.

16. The relative length and elaborateness of this temptation seem to be without precedent.

17. This technique is studied further in "In Order Serviceable," a study of the *Nativity Ode* forthcoming in *MLR.*

18. *P.L.,* VI, 472.

19. *Dan.* 11, 35 and *Dan.* IV, 11 are customarily cited but *Matt.* 20, 44 is not without its relevance and Donne's typical exposition of this double-edged text (Simpson and Potter, *ed. cit.,* Vol. IV, 180–96) is instructive in putting before us the relationship between what the audience does know and what Satan cannot know.

20. The repudiation of Athens is distressing to many because if Christ is perfect man undergoing the temptations in his human aspect, his "rejections" become examples which we are inexorably called on to follow. One way out is to suggest that what Christ says is relative to the context of argument: thus Socrates can be commended in one place and the limits of his knowledge severely exposed in another. The basic difficulty can also be bypassed by suggesting that we are not inescapably called on to follow Christ's example at all points. This is the effect of Howard Schultz's view that Christ as head of the church puts forward counsels of perfection meant "not primarily for the Christian layman but for the Church and its ministers," (*Milton and Forbidden Knowledge,* New York, 1955, p. 233). The view suggested in the present article is that while Christ may be perfect man, he is also the historic Christ, exhibiting in his responses an emerging awareness of his destiny. Such a way of reading is not implausible and by adopting it we would enrich substantially the poem's natural ironies.

21. *P.R.,* IV, 235.

22. *Comus,* 707. *P.L.* 11, 564.

23. *P.R.,* IV, 352.

24. That Christ's rejections are not ultimately rejections is suggested by III, 433–40 and by the saving "yet" in IV, 131. Once again the play is between the reader's knowledge of Christ's transforming mission, Christ's emerging knowledge of it, and Satan's ignorance.

THE METAPHOR OF INSPIRATION IN *PARADISE LOST*

John T. Shawcross

Inspiration is literally a breathing into, and for Milton as Christian poet it is the breathing of the *anima* of God into him as mortal. Such "animation" supplies the life-giving force which will bring about creation. For the poet the result is his poem. Theologically inspiration implies divine action which will enlighten mortal mind to receive divine truth. The poet's creation thus inspired will present the truth which is God: it will be an emblem of God's own creation. So viewed, *Paradise Lost* becomes the creation of God and Milton, its subject matter offering comparison and contrast between God's creation of Heaven and the universe and Hell, and what Man can make of his world if he is inspired by God or if he is perverted by Satan. Should Man receive the inspiration of God, his world will reflect Heaven and there will be a paradise within; a form of unity will ensue. Should he succumb to the perversions of Satan, his world will reflect Hell and he will be a hell himself; a form of nonunity will ensue.

The need for joint action between God and man is explicit in *Sonnet 7* as well as other early poems. But the basic equation which underlies the preceding remarks is the mystic union of God

and Man in terms of sexual intercourse. One need remember
only Donne's famous sonnet, "Batter my heart, three person'd
God," to realize the prevalence of this metaphor. The metaphor
figures the spirit (*anima*) of God as the dynamic, creative, fiery
male force and the receiver of God's spirit as the passive, dormant, cold female factor. Union, as in intercourse, will create,
the opposites being fused into that which partakes of both: a
poem dominated by mortal action but imbued with divine truth.
Such metaphor derives from natural observation, from alchemi-
cal experiment with sulphur and mercury, from the age-old para-
digm of earth-fire-air-water, even from the mystic properties of
bread and wine. It is common to mystic expression such as that of
St. Teresa of Avila. In *Paradise Lost* Milton employs this metaphor, as we shall see, with a complexity of meaning and application that encompasses all areas of Man's life. The epic is itself a
creation which discusses on various levels creation as it occurred
in orthodox belief, as it occurs each day in Man and to Man,
both bodily and conceptually, and as it will occur in the ultimate
union at the end of time. With the War on Earth at an end, so
that God will be All in All (III, 339–341; VI, 730–732; 1 Cor.
xv.28), worthy man will be "reduced" to God by Michael (who
is related to Hermes as guide of the dead) just as he led back the
faithful angels "Under thir Head imbodied all in one" (VI, 779)
at the end of the War in Heaven. In this apocalyptic vision, the
imbodiment of all in God, the One, is necessary for full return
from *ex Deo* creation, and it implies in the context of the metaphor we have been examining an unending coition.[1] Here the
colloquial meaning of the word "die" as sexual intercourse becomes significant, for "to the faithful Death [will be] the Gate of
Life" (XII, 571).[2]

The proem to book one of *Paradise Lost* (lines 1–26) ad-
dresses first the "Heav'nly Muse" who inspired Moses on Horeb
or Sinai. Who is addressed has been under discussion for a
number of years; see Merritt Y. Hughes' full survey of the matter
in *SEL*, IV (1964), 1–33, and the most recent argument, that

of William B. Hunter, Jr., immediately following on pp. 35–42. As the present essay proposes, I believe that the spirit of God, at least, is invoked, regardless of which specific person of the Trinity is intended. Moses was typologically identified with the Son in his role as prophet (here expressed as shepherd, a role the poet plays for his readers), and Exodus iii tells of how God spoke to him on Mt. Horeb, and Exodus xix, how God spoke to him on Mt. Sinai. First God inspires Moses, who has protested that he is not eloquent but slow of speech and tongue (iv.10), by being with his mouth and teaching him what to say (iv.12).[3] Moses is to lead the chosen people forth from bondage, as we deduce Milton hopes to lead forth his fellowmen from the bondage of Sin through his poem. Later, on Mt. Sinai, God speaks the words of the laws (including the ten commandments) which will keep his covenant and make the Israelites his peculiar treasure above all people. Milton too elaborates the law of God throughout and specifically by reference to the Son's example:

> The Law of God exact he shall fulfill
> Both by obedience and by love, though love
> Alone fulfill the Law;   (XII, 402–404)

Next the "Heav'nly Muse" is invoked by virtue of her inspiration at Zion (2 Samuel vii). David, ancestor of Jesus, king of the Israelites and thus typologically identified with the Son in his role as King, wished to build a temple for God's ark of covenant. The word of the Lord came to Nathan, the prophet, that David's act would be rewarded by his seed's establishment of a kingdom to last forever: "I will be his father, and he shall be my son" (vii.14). The importance of the Son and the Son as Man to the whole of *Paradise Lost* has only in recent years been recognized, but here is another allusion (following soon after that to the "one greater Man" in 1.4), not only to the Son but to the apocalypse. In a way, I suppose, Milton's poem becomes his temple for God's covenant. Or contrasting with "Sion Hill" the Muse's aid is invoked by her presence at the brook of Siloam, which flowed by the temple in Jerusalem, identified with David's temple on Zion. Here the reference is to John ix, in which Jesus heals the blind man by anointing his eyes with clay and having him wash in the pool of Siloam. The role of priest—Jesus said, "I must work the works of him that sent me, while it is day: the night cometh, when no man can work" (ix.4)—underlies the reference and again points to apocalypse. Clay is a symbol of mortality, and the biblical message is that we are all blind until we have experienced the trials of being mortal and have then bathed ourselves in the spirituality of God's Logos ("the Oracle of God"). For Milton, the blind man, the allusion had special significance, as seen when he asks the Spirit to illumine that which is dark within him (I. 22–23) and when we remember that the blind man is blind, not because he has sinned or because his parents have sinned, but in order that the works of God should be made manifest in him (ix.3). The concept of knowing good by knowing evil, of the development of a paradise fairer far after the fall, is hinted at in this allusion to Siloam.

We see in these few lines an appeal to the Heavenly Muse to inspire the poet so that he can function as prophet, king, and priest of God's Word in order that he may manifest the works of God in his poem. Should he be so inspired, he will have asserted Eternal Providence and thereby have justified to men the ways of God toward men. Like Moses he hopes to teach how order comes out of chaos, light out of darkness, good out of evil, in his poem, through his imagery, and even through himself as the enlightened blind man. The suggestion in the reference to the blind man healed, that one must first be mortal—that is, fallen—before God's truth can be meaningful, is underscored first by the poet's appeal that the spirit raise and support that which is low within him, for Milton himself is fallen man; second, by his beginning in the darkness and evil of Hell; third, by Michael's words and Adam's realizations in XII; and fourth, by the sexual imagery of supine Man awaiting God's inspiration.

Milton calls on the Spirit of God, who seems to be another

aspect of the Heavenly Muse by the continued and unspecified use of the polite second person into lines 27 ff. The temple of Zion, cited just before, has led to invocation of the Spirit, for God prefers "th'upright heart and pure" before temples: "Know ye not that ye are the temple of God, and that the Spirit of God dwelleth in you?" (1 Cor. iii.16); "know ye not that your body is the temple of the Holy Ghost which is in you, which ye have of God, and ye are not your own?" (1 Cor. vi.19); "Lord, who shall abide in thy tabernacle? who shall dwell in thy holy hill? / He that walketh uprightly, and worketh righteousness, and speaketh the truth in his heart" (Ps. xv.1–2); "The way of the just is uprightness: thou, most upright, dost weigh the path of the just" (Isa. xxvi.7). Through the probable allusion to Isaiah we see the relationship between the upright heart and justification of God's ways. The Spirit is seen as a dove-like creature which stretches out its wings and sits on the vast abyss (Chaos) and impregnates it. In summary we have the main motif of the poem: out of chaos will be created the universe (in VII), out of evil will come good, out of darkness will come light (throughout the poem and especially as we move from II to III, and in the illumination of the blind poet and his blind readers), out of disordered elements will come dove-like creatures (men who have been engendered by the Spirit of God). Perhaps we should also note that the dove was a symbol of the Holy Ghost, and of course it is a white creature that will emerge from black elements. The infusion of God as male force on the dormant and womb-like abyss is the cosmic parallel of the besought infusion of God on the receptive poet, as the colon after "pregnant" indicates. The poet is paralleled with the abyss, and the sexual imagery of the later appertains to the poet. Milton's poem will hopefully also produce dove-like creatures—will, that is, if he can assert Eternal Providence to man's understanding. Justification of God's ways will ensue if Milton can demonstrate God's love for Man and if he can help bring Man to love God (with its implications of faith in God and therefore obedience to God). Since love is, I believe, the theme of the poem, it is natural that a basic image pattern derive from the nature of love, and that the perversion of love of God derive from the nature of sexual perversion shown in the Satanic parodies.

The lines referring to the dove-like creature are drawn from the gospels' discussion of Jesus's baptism[4] (Matt. iii.16; Mark i.10; Luke iii.22; John i.32), and we should note that each declares Jesus as Son of God. Those who are thus generated, we deduce, will be sons of God and thus worthy of return to God at the end of mortal time. But Milton as hopeful poet surely also thought of the descent of the dove to the apostles, who then "began to speak with other tongues, as the Spirit gave them utterance" (Acts ii.4), and probably of the psalmist's wish for "wings like a dove" to "fly away, and be at rest" (lv.6). Only the dove-like creature will be able to soar to heaven and find his eternal rest. The narrator is portrayed as a bird throughout the poem, and he must surely be a dove-like being, created by God's inspirational infusion of his dark and blind self.

The poet as bird has been explored by Anne Davidson Ferry in *Reason and the Imagination* (N.Y., 1962), pp. 183–200, and *Milton's Epic Voice* (Harvard Univ. Press, 1963). Perhaps, however, we should note that in dream psychology a bird and flying have sensual significance: flying dreams are erection dreams, hovering signifying erotic experience, and falling, erotic temptation accompanied by anxiety. That Milton's work is a "dream"—not only in the sense of a divine vision with apocalyptic revelation—is emphasized by his frequent citation of nightly inspiration: "Nightly I visit . . . as the wakeful Bird / Sings darkling, and in shadiest Covert hid / Tunes her nocturnal Note" (III, 32, 38–40); "yet not alone, while thou / Visit'st my slumbers Nightly, or when Morn / Purples the East" (VII, 28–30); "my Celestial Patroness, who deignes / Her nightly visitation unimplor'd, / And dictates to me slumbring, or inspires / Easie my unpremeditated Verse . . . who brings it nightly to my Ear" (IX, 21–24, 47). Of course part of his night is his blindness as the proem to III shows. But the psychological implications of his "dream-poem," if we may call it that,[5] are consonant with the sexual imagery used in the bird image of the first proem, and thus are worthy of citation. Certainly there are sections in which the poet's ascent, flight, and descent are explicit. The creational relationship between the Spirit of God (as male force but presented as female inspirer) and the poet (as female factor but presented in terms of dream psychology as male) is conveyed by the flight of the bird-narrator through the auspices of the Spirit from the depths of Hell through Chaos and Ancient Night to the heights of Heaven to the reality of Earth, followed by fluctuations of flight though based on Earth and extended in XI and XII beyond the climax of IX and X. In XI and XII we have the birth which will ensue from Adam and Eve's seduction, but in the poem itself we have the birth which will ensue from the divine rapture of the poet by the Spirit of God. As the bird-narrator descends in IV we have statements of anxiety, although the earthly fall is only foreseen in that book; they are stronger in the proem to IX, in which the earthly fall will actually take place. The anxiety of the proem of the seventh book is for the poet himself, lest he not be inspired further by the Spirit. The implication in his calling Calliope, muse of heroic poetry, but an empty dream[6] is that his dream-poem, inspired by God, is worthwhile and will not prove sterile. Continued inspiration only will bring birth, and so the ensuing birth, out of the watery abyss, is that of the created universe itself, then of man, then of woman. When we reach IX, anxiety for self again arises, for decay or cold or age may depress the narrator's wing, should the Spirit of God desert him. Such depression of flight implies the denial of erotic experience and the impossibility of creation at this point of climax. Without relation of the climactic point of the stated subject of the poem, Man's disobedience, the insemination of the poet's "message" by inspiration of the Spirit would not take place.

The "message" is finally delivered in X (originally and perhaps significantly IX in the first edition of 1667): the Son's judgment looking forward to the Incarnation and ultimately to the Last Judgment preceding the return to God makes clear what God's Providence is—His Son—and why His ways are just. The remaining two books (a single book in 1667) delineate resolution for the poem and the poet with the conclusion that death can be the gate of life and with the desiccating imagery of the final lines of the poem. At the same time these books depict the cyclic generation which Adam and Eve's disobedience has begot. Hopefully there will also be some dove-like creatures born of Milton's poem.

The nightly visitation of Milton's inspiring Muse has two additional associations: First, there is the implied allusion to Asmodai in Tobit, "the fleshliest Incubus," who killed Tobias' wife's first seven husbands, referred to at IV, 167–171; V, 221–223; and VI, 362–368. Asmodai was a fallen angel, infamous as a demonic nightly visitor, who seduced his victims by taking the guise of the true husband. Only Raphael, "the medicine of God," as the name means in Hebrew, is able to vanquish him. Here is an obverse example of the poet's nightly visitation, one that emphasizes sexuality and lustfulness. It becomes another instance of distorted mirror surfaces in the poem. The differences between the love-making of Adam and Eve in IV and IX indicate the potential difficulties that the dreamer may encounter. The nature of these opposing nightly visits is echoed in Satan's visit to Eve as she sleeps in IV (related in V) and in God's presence in Eve's dream in XII. In the latter case the visitation to Eve takes place during the day, thus suggesting Milton's constant night even during the day. This association reinforces the metaphor of inspiration in *Paradise Lost* and makes clear the difference between good and evil in such matters. Second, there is the underlying belief that God cannot visit Man directly, but only through one of His aspects, as Jove visited Semele. When Jove visited her as a God (the myth is an accommodation of the idea that he who sees God must die), she was consumed by his lightning. However, we again see the metaphor in operation. Milton has learned the way of the teacher: "And I, brethren, could not speak unto you as unto spiritual, but as unto carnal, even as unto babes in Christ" (1 Cor. iii.1). As Joseph Summers has commented, ". . . the desire for sexual fulfilment is itself considered a symbol for or a sublimation of the more primary human desire for union with God" (op. cit., p. 111).

As I read *Paradise Lost,* therefore, I am struck by the metaphor of inspiration with its sexual overtones: the poem itself is the creation of God and the poet; it simulates an act of generation through psychological motif, subject matter, strategically placed proems, and rhythm; it deals with creation which is bodily, conceptual, and physical; and it suggests constant generation through impregnation of its readers with its "message." Milton has written a poem which makes viable Isaiah's words: "With my soul have I desired thee in the night; yea, with my spirit within me will seek thee early: for when thy judgments are in the earth, the inhabitatants of the world will learn righteousness" (xxvi.9). Just as some of Adam and Eve's progeny fall, so some readers will not receive the inspiration of the work—which like God's created universe holds all (then) available knowledge, all that one needs for "life"; but some will be fit audience though few. "God is also in sleep, and Dreams advise" (XII, 611), says Eve, and so now awake with God's judgment of restoration before them, she and Adam accept Providence as their guide (as should each reader). As they wipe the few natural tears from their eyes, the final resurrection of soul is suggested, for "God shall wipe alway all tears from their eyes, and there shall be no more death, neither sorrow, nor crying, neither shall there be any more pain: for the former things are passed away" (Rev. xxi.4).

University of Wisconsin

NOTES

1. Though the Father is male force, this imbodiment sees God as the Great Mother, his sons returning to the womb. Both the circle of perfection which God represents (although Heaven is square) and the Eternal Garden, as Heaven is described, are symbols of the mother archetype, according to Jung. But we should remember that the father is seen as energy; the mother, as form. This, I believe, explains the sexual ambivalences within the poem. See also Joseph Summers excellent discussion of "The Two Great Sexes" in *The Muse's Method* (London, 1963), pp. 87–111.

2. We should note the infernal parody which is implied throughout. The unfaithful couple with Sin, Satan's "perfect image," through her enticing them "with attractive graces," and they beget monstrous things, like the Hell Hounds which kennel themselves in her womb (II, 653–659). Whereas God inspires, Sin entices bodily and, it is implied, through such narcissism as that by which Satan has fallen. This is the reason behind Raphael's perturbation in VIII, 561 ff., when Adam, in a preview of what will cause his fall in IX, says that all higher knowledge falls degraded in Eve's presence: she is flesh of his flesh, bone of his bone, his image before him. A sexual note is also struck by Sin's description as "a Serpent arm'd With mortal sting," for not only is a serpent a phallic symbol, here transferred to the woman because she is the aggressor and the entire context suggests perversion, but the words "arm'd" and "mortal" and "sting" all involve sexual puns. The nonunity, or rather annihilation of being, which unfaithfulness will yield appears not only in the image of the Hell Hounds gnawing their Mother's bowels (in contrast with everlasting life in unity with God), but in the resplendent throne of pearl and gold on which Satan sits in Pandemonium: Freud showed that gold was considered the excrement of hell, that gold and treasure were equated with defecation, and that defecation dreams, with feces piled high, represented the death wish. The irony of Satan's wishing for death, which this throne as psychological symbol implies (though death-wish is also clear from his soliloquy in IV, 71–78, 86–102), lies in his begetting Death with Sin, in his abhorrence of Death, in the Son's redemption of Man to make death the gate of life, and thus in the ambivalent metaphoric meaning of the word "die."

3. Interestingly God gives Moses a rod by which to show His divinity through miracle, and the rod, of course, becomes a serpent when dashed to the ground. As we read *Paradise Lost* we should remember the serpent

as phallic symbol, the earth as female symbol, and chaste engagement in sex as productive of the miracle of life. Only through the sexual perversion of Satan as serpent seducing Eve in the Garden does this beast of the fields become evil symbol. The positive virtues of sex (as seen, for example, in IV) have too often been overlooked in this poem.

4. Water is a symbol both of spirituality and of birth. As rain, water is male; as standing water, such as an ocean, it is female. That Milton refers to an aqueous abyss in this line is evident from its echo in VII, 233–237 ("Darkness profound / Cover'd th' Abyss: but on the watrie calm / His brooding wings the Spirit of God outspread, / And vital vertue infus'd, and vital warmth / Throughout the fluid Mass") and from its early version in the *Nativity Ode,* 68 ("While Birds of Calm sit brooding on the charmed wave"). This latter reference to the halcyons' breeding in December and around the time of the nativity of the Son as Man is of course most significant as another indication of the constant presence of the Son in *Paradise Lost.* Those who follow the Son, who is imbued at his baptism with the Spirit of God, will be dove-like creatures and saved; surely a main point of the poem is to counsel men to follow the example of the Son in his love and obedience. Lines 9–13 of III also reprise these lines of I: "and at the voice / of God, as with a Mantle didst invest / The rising world of waters dark and deep,/Won from the void and formless infinite."

5. Dreams reduce antitheses to uniformity or at least represent them as one and the same thing. The polarities of God and Satan in *Paradise Lost* which have often been pointed out, organize into mirror surfaces of each other, becoming another factor in the dream-vision nature of the poem.

6. The reference to Calliope's son Orpheus, the archetypal poet, who was beheaded by drunken Bacchantes, has two functions: it primarily notices that the accommodation of heavenly truth in such popular myths as this of the resurrection of Christ are ineffectual (as opposed to what Milton hopes to achieve by his more direct and unaccommodated use of myth); and it intimates the emasculation of heavenly truth delivered by "Harp and Voice" which lustfulness can bring.

PARADISE LOST
AND THE ITALIAN EPIC
TRADITION

Wayne Shumaker

What is not present in a work of literary art is less often studied than what is present. This is natural enough, for when we observe an object we do not instinctively tell ourselves that it is not made of such-and-such materials or lacks such-and-such formal qualities. Only a specialist is likely to notice that in a Renaissance painting of the Annunciation Mary is not identified with Second Eve by the presence of an apple in the background, or to wonder about the rejection in *King Lear* of the happy ending that Shakespeare found in all his sources. An extended literary work like *Paradise Lost,* especially, is rich enough to hold attention for a long time within its boundaries; and when curiosity invites us to examine its context, we hunt rather for what relates to it directly than for what quite clearly is different. Nevertheless a work is what it is quite as much because of exclusions as because of admissions. The lack of reflective depth in Hemingway's novels, or of sharp visual details in Auden's poetry, is by no means critically negligible. In what follows, I propose to discuss certain epic precedents that Milton chose not to follow. The result, I hope, will be a slightly fuller understanding, and perhaps also a somewhat livelier appreciation, of his achievement in *Paradise Lost.*

When, in the middle 1650's, Milton at last began serious work on the epic he had so long aspired to write, he either decided against or, more probably, did not bother to reconsider the Arthurian subject which for a time had attracted him. His distrust of the Arthurian legends, manifested emphatically in the third book of his *History of Britain* ("But who *Arthur* was, and whether ever any such reign'd in *Britain,* hath bin doubted heertofore, and may again with good reason"[1]), is well known; but the full implications of the rejection have not so far as I know, been drawn out. For, with Arthur, Milton apparently rejected a chivalric subject; and with that, in turn, he rejected the only epic tradition, along with its subject-matter and machinery, which during a century and a half of eager experimentation by European poets had shown itself capable of generating epics which could win both popularity and critical esteem.

The tradition, of course, was that initiated by Boiardo somewhat stumblingly in his *Orlando Innamorato* (1495), developed brilliantly by Ariosto in *Orlando Furioso* (1516; revised and expanded in 1532), deprived of its humor and given a deeper seriousness by Tasso in *Gerusalemme Liberata* (1581), and imported into England, with an elaboration of "darke conceits," by Spenser's *Faerie Queene.* No other option had proved itself equally viable: the prose pastoral of Sidney's *Arcadia;* the epic of "true" history, with notes and references, attempted by Daniel in his *Civil Wars;* Drayton's geographical *Poly-Olbion;* the "witty" Biblical *Davideis* of Cowley, very near to *Paradise Lost* in point of time; the epic of classical subject-matter—Leonard Digges' *The Rape of Proserpine* or Shakerley Marmion's *Cupid and Psyche;* the divine allegory of Edward Benlowes' *Theophila;* the expansively baroque *Sepmaines divines* of Du Bartas, initially admired but soon repudiated as "classical" standards won ground in France; or any other of the astonishingly varied forms between Petrarch's *Africa* and Davenant's *Gondibert,* so diverse and yet all apparently intended as epics. Except perhaps for the *Arcadia,* now usually read as pastoral romance and not as prose epic, most of these are now known chiefly by title—except, indeed, that a university instructor may occasionally describe a few of them in a lecture on "The Epic Background of *Paradise Lost*" to illustrate the Renaissance thirst for a literary fame thought to be attainable only through the writing of epic. The Italian "romantic" or "ir-regular" epic had succeeded, however, so resoundingly that the *Orlando Furioso* attained some two hundred European editions in the eighty-four years after its first publication; and Milton's repudiation of the model excluded him from one inviting area of possibility.

In 1642 Milton had still held the area open. Hoping, he says in the preface to the second book of *The Reason of Church Government,* to "leave something so written to aftertimes, as they should not willingly let it die," he had weighed sympathetically what he then regarded as the two chief formal possibilities: "whether that Epick form whereof the two poems of *Homer,* and those other two of *Virgil* and *Tasso* are a diffuse, and the book of *Job* a brief model: or whether the rules of *Aristotle* herein are strictly to be kept, or nature to be follow'd, which in them that know art, and use judgement is no transgression, but an enrich-ing of art."[2] The last clause offers a defense of the Italian epic on the grounds that it is closer to nature—a respectable argument based on the standard Aristotelian principle that art is mimetic. By the 1650's, however, he had brought himself to relinquish the privilege of irregularity; and the decision had major conse-quences.

It meant, first of all, the choice of a simple rather than a complex—"complex," here, on a scale too huge to be suggested briefly. All three of the Italian epics, but especially those of Boiardo and Ariosto, had been so intricately plotted that efforts to summarize them regularly emphasize two or three selected strands and ignore, or making despairing gestures toward, the rest. One measure of the complexity is that one hundred sixteen personal names are listed under the single letter "A" in an index appended to John Hoole's eighteenth-century translation of the *Furioso*.[3] A calculation based on the first ten pages of the sixty-four page index suggests that the total number of personages actually mentioned in the poem is approximately seven hundred forty-eight. The variety of actions required to involve so many characters—even when allowance is made for those merely mentioned, as in a catalogue of knights, or alluded to—is necessarily great, and the epic is very long. By my count, the *Furioso* contains 38,632 lines and perhaps a quarter of a million words against the 10,565 lines, or roughly twenty-seven percent of the number, in *Paradise Lost*. Even the shortest of the three poems, the *Gerusalemme Liberata,* strains the memory. An index to my Italian edition[4] lists seventy-four personal names under "A"; on the same basis as before, we can expect to find some four hundred seventy-three characters active or alluded to in the entire work. In reading the *Furioso,* moreover, one must begin with a knowledge of Boiardo's *Innamorato* (or at least find out somehow what has happened in it) and then, from point to point, remember details from several, or many, cantos back. Not merely the characters, but also many of the physical properties, have histories: the swords Durindana and Balisarda, a suit of armor originally worn by Hector and later by Mandricardo and Ruggiero, a golden lance carried, in turn, by Argalia (calling himself Uberto), Astolfo, and Bradamante. The horses Baiardo, Rabicano, Frontino, and Brigliadoro also have backgrounds. As the references lead all the way back to the Trojan War, they carry forward, by prophecies, clear to the time of Ariosto's patron the Cardinal Ippolito d'Este. By the time the reader closes the final volume of Ariosto he should be able, if only his head did not whirl so, to people roughly twenty-seven hundred years rather thickly with real and fictive persons and to trace whole genealogical lines almost from the beginning, with a proper discrimination of collateral branches and an understanding of the relationships among ruling families. All this, however, comes at him piecemeal

and sometimes obscured by disguises, so that the disentangling of
the various strands and the patterning of all the actions would be
a work akin to Father Ronald Knox's drawing a map of Trol-
lope's Barsetshire from hints dropped in the novels.

Nothing short of a first-hand reading can make what has been
said very meaningful; but the nature of the complexity, and also
perhaps something of the intellectual and psychological tone of
the epic universe, can be hinted by a summary of the way in
which one line of action begins. The real hero of the *Furioso* is
rather Ruggiero than the title-character, Orlando (the Roland of
the Old French *Chanson de Roland,* though not described here in
relation to the fight at Roncevaux). This Ruggiero was the leg-
endary founder of the house of Este, to which, as has been said,
Ariosto's patron belonged. The ultimate forebear of the line was
the Trojan Astyanax, son of Hector; but Ruggiero's father, also
named Ruggiero, was a descendant of the French king Clovis (d.
511) and therefore a kinsman of Charlemagne. The Ruggiero
of the *Furioso* had been a posthumous child, and (we have been
told by Boiardo), his mother dying soon after his birth, he was
reared by Atlante, a magician who because of a threatening
prophecy had confined him to an enchanted castle. The pagan
armies now attacking Charlemagne's realm had wished to obtain
his help—he is not yet a Christain, although he is ultimately to
become one to marry the Christian heroine Bradamante—and
they had succeeded in discovering the castle with the aid of
Angelica's magical ring, which, when worn on the finger, as we
have learned in the earlier poem, protects against enchantments,
or, when placed in the mouth, makes the bearer invisible. This
ring, Boiardo has informed us, had been stolen by a despicable
knight named Brunello, who at the same time had stolen Sacri-
pante's horse, Frontino; Orlando's sword, Balisarda (earlier won
from the enchantress Falerina); and Orlando's famous horn,
which petrifies with fear anyone who hears it. Well, this Ruggiero, to come back to Ariosto. . . . If by this point the listener is
already becoming confused, the narrator has been driven to

hopelessness by his failure to make progress. In comparison with the involutions and expatiations of the *Orlando* materials, Congreve's *Way of the World* is a compact little anecdote and Tolstoy's *War and Peace* refreshingly unilinear. The nearest English parallel would be not so much Spenser's *Faerie Queene* as the entire Arthurian cycle, French and English; or perhaps, in recent literature, J. R. R. Tolkien's *The Lord of the Rings* together with *The Hobbit* and all the "historical" excerpts and genealogies printed at the end of *The Rings,* as the *lacunae* in these had been pieced out by generations of conjecture and straightforward fictive invention.

In comparison, *Paradise Lost* is like Racine's *Britannicus* (1669), with its seven clearly delineated characters and sharply posed issues. Racine had chosen for his play "une action simple, chargée de peu de matière, telle que doit être une action qui se passe en un seul jour"; some of his critics would have preferred it to be filled "de quantité d'incidents qui ne se pourroient passer qu'en un mois, d'un grand nombre de jeux de théâtre d'autant plus surprenants qu'ils seroient moins vraisemblables, d'une infinité de déclamations" (*Première préface*). Fondness for the old-fashioned horizontal elaboration resisted, in some quarters, the new tendency to explore vertically; but in post-Restoration culture generally, in both France and England, a centripetal tug was gradually to replace the explosive centrifugal energy of the Renaissance proper.

Paradise Lost remains, of course, baroque. Only by the exercise of an almost superhuman control is the action kept within its frame, temporally and cosmically vast as that is. Milton's epic none the less has a focus that was new in epic and nearly as new in narrative. The older tendency to multiply incidents instead of exploring a problem appears clearly in most narration from Homer and Virgil, through such a protracted "novel" as *The Golden Ass* of Lucius Apuleius, clear down to and beyond Defoe's *Moll Flanders. Paradise Lost* thus signalizes a movement toward the thematic simplicity of Richardson's *Pamela* or—once more to take a twentieth-century example—Wharton's *Ethan Frome,* where a few characters are etched sharply and in deep relief against a richly rendered background. If much was lost, much also was gained—most significantly, penetration. The world was becoming too complicated for writers to confront more than a chosen segment at one time.

A second rejection was of what can loosely be called magic. Although this choice too marks an advance toward modernity, what it involved can again be described only with the aid of examples.

No reader of Homer or Virgil can have failed to notice how many of the actions have their real causes outside of human will and social circumstances. From the sending of the plague upon the Greeks by Apollo to the very end, the gods direct spears, snatch away endangered favorites, rouse the spirits of warriors, inspire dread, appear to human beings in disguise, and otherwise influence events. In Virgil, the role of religious ritual is astonishingly great. No important action is undertaken without preliminary sacrifices, and much of the narrative interest depends upon the fulfillment of prophecies. Virgil himself was no less pious than his hero, and his piety motivated a demonstration that Rome's imperial destiny was divinely fated. In the Italian Renaissance epics, what in the ancient masterpieces seems to us an intellectually benighted, if humanly fascinating, view of the world degenerates (I speak from a modern bias) into blatant and vulgar magic.

A few illustrations must serve for many. Mention has already been made of Angelica's ring, the magician Atlante, and Orlando's horn. These marvels are symptomatic: cut across the narrative at any angle and you will find it larded with wonders. The vicissitudes of Rinaldo's love-affair with Angelica are caused by draughts from one or the other of two springs produced earlier by Merlin, one of which induces love and the other hate. A griffin-horse carries two knights on separate world-tours. Astolfo is transformed to a myrtle tree. Rodomonte wears an invulnerable serpent skin, Orlando's natural skin—like Achilles'—is impervious to weapons, and Hector's armor, worn successively by Mandricardo and Ruggiero, is similarly invulnerable. The swords Durindana and Balisarda are irresistible. A shield carried for a time by Ruggiero so dazzles the sight of enemies that, in order to avoid having an unfair advantage, he throws it at last into a deep well. The sorceress Alcina charms men who attract her by enticing them into an enchanted garden. Two beneficent magicians, Melissa and Malagigi, accomplish their designs by constraining the service of daemons. All this in Boiardo and Ariosto; but in the more religious Tasso the situation is not different. (I disregard here the later—and unsuccessful—version called *Gerusalemme Conquistata,* which, as the *Enciclopedia Italiana* notes, strives for "una logica esterna e fredda.") The chief obstacle to Goffredo di Buglione's conquest of Jerusalem is the placing of an enchantment on the only forest from which wood can be obtained for necessary assault towers. In the end Rinaldo, who for a time has been engaged in amorous dalliance with the enchantress Armida on an island to which he has been magically transported, is rescued in a magical boat, walks unharmed through a wall of magical fire, strides to a great tree at the center of the wood, and belabors it with his sword, whereupon it turns out to be the very Armida whom he has just left on the island. The sorcery is thus lifted and the Christians are enabled to proceed with their attack. Earlier, Armida has enticed a number of the doughtiest Christians to a charmed castle, where they are detained for a time by her spells. So also, though with differences that I dare not attempt to analyze, in Spenser.

Now what is most interesting about this magic is that very likely it is not, like improbabilities in most recent fiction, mere belletristic ornament intended to excite wonder. The chances are rather strong that Boiardo, Ariosto, and—less certainly—Tasso in some sense *believed* in magic and thought that it played an important role in human affairs. Not, of course, that the specific marvels appeared to the authors as Truth. Ariosto is often amused by his prodigies. The point is that all three wrote at a time when the most highly educated and intelligent men in Europe were convinced that the world is permeated with occult forces which operate constantly upon the universe of human experience in ways hidden from the uninitiated.

The subject is a complicated and obscure one which I hope to explore at another time in a full volume. Here I can only try to suggest that the opinion just offered is not wild. On the contrary, it is supported by much recent investigation of magic, astrology, alchemy, demonology, witchcraft, and, not least important, the Hermetic tradition. Since the publication of a notable study by R. Reitzenstein in 1904,[5] a body of notions stemming, allegedly, from a Hermes Trismegistus roughly contemporary with Moses has been brilliantly analyzed by a handful of superbly equipped specialists[6] whose findings have begun to infiltrate Renaissance scholarship. Evidence is accumulating steadily that, from Ficino to Francis Bacon, some of the most enlightened minds in Italy, France, Germany, and England took very seriously a hodgepodge of magical beliefs already evident in Plato's *Timaeus* but most widely disseminated in the second and third centuries after the birth of Christ. The discovery is surprising and, to me at least, unwelcome. I should prefer to believe that the human mind had made consistent intellectual progress. The facts, however, as they become increasingly available, make skepticism more and more difficult.

Some of the evidence is already known to Renaissance specialists. It has long been recognized, for example, that the sixteenth and seventeenth centuries were the heyday of witchcraft and that an interest in judicial astrology was widespread. The assertion of Paul H. Kocher that those who "spoke up for astrology" in the Elizabethan period were "chiefly the foremost scientific men of the age" may, however, be unexpected.[7] (The chief opponents were clergymen.) Giordano Bruno, long celebrated as a martyr to inductive science, has been proved by Frances A. Yates[8] to have been basically a magician. Ficino's translation of the first four-

teen books of the *Corpus Hermeticum* into Latin had, we are told
by P. O. Kristeller,[9] such an "immense diffusion" that more
manuscripts of it exist than of any other writing by Ficino; and
Ficino himself was drawn by the task into a deep interest in
magical talismans. His friend Pico della Mirandola, according to
Yates, not only also used cabalistic magic and attempted to
constrain the aid of daemons but in his *Città del Sole* (written
about 1602) explained how to make the citizens of an ideal state
perfectly virtuous and healthy by setting magical images around
the walls—an idea borrowed, apparently, from a curious document called the *Picatrix,* in which a city called Adocentyn, pro-
tected by just such images, is said to have been built by Hermes.[10]
Not even Copernicus's skirts are wholly free: "he had quoted,
near his diagram of the new system, Hermes Trismegistus in the
Asclepius on the sun as the visible god."[11] The comparatively late
Rosicrucianism may have had a Hermetic source, and so too,
although the evidence here is less persuasive, may Freemasonry.
So far I have been drawing chiefly upon Yates; but the fullest and
most sympathetic account of magic known to me, the *Occulta
Philosophia* of Cornelius Agrippa of Nettesheim (written about
1510; first published in 1531), also dates from this period. As
late as 1656, when Milton was presumably already engaged on
his epic, the *Corpus* was printed in an English translation by
John Evrard with a preface by J[oseph] F[isher] claiming that
Hermes, who "lived in the time of *Sarug, Abrahams* great
Grand-Father," was "the greatest Philosopher, and therefore the
greatest Divine":[12] and this long after the explosion by Isaac
Casaubon, in 1614, of the claim that the *Corpus* had its origin
in remote Egyptian antiquity. But these details are the merest
samplings.

   Milton, it need hardly be said, has little use for magic. For the
Visible God (the cosmos) of the Hermetics, their thirty-six dec-
ans, the twelve signs of the zodiac with their "houses," the
intimate "sympathies" of minerals, plants, and animals with
heavenly bodies, their talismans, and, most importantly of all

perhaps, their omnipresent *daimones,* he substituted God and His
angels. If the Miltonic universe differs from that of modern
science by reason of its permeation with divine benevolence,
happenings in it are not determined by astrological influence, and
no suggestion is offered that the way to get things done is to put
magical constraints on occult forces. The advice given Adam by
Raphael not to trouble his head much about cosmology ("Sollicit
not thy thoughts with matters hid, / Leave them to God above,
him serve and feare"—VIII, 167–68), although it relates most
immediately to frivolous astronomical speculation, may well reflect a distaste for the star-gazing still practiced by astrologists of
Milton's period. To be sure, fallen angels—devils—exist for Milton as well as the Father and Son; and all the supernal spirits may
appear vestigially magical. On the whole, however, the universe
of *Paradise Lost* is infinitely clearer, saner, and simpler than the
necromantic one of his Italian predecessors. "Influence" has been
replaced by human responsibility. The magical properties, as
well, are mostly gone (though one remembers Ithuriel's spear in
Book IV), and no meteorological or animal auspices sig-
nal—and hence require—the impending tragedy. Perhaps the
intellectual trouble of some modern readers, indeed, stems from
their reluctant perception that Milton's universe just might "take
in" less happily sophisticated minds.

Finally, the ruling interests in Milton's epic world are not
those operative among the Italian: valor, honor, and romantic
love. (Of these, the last was mostly foreign to Homer and Virgil
and was rejected decisively in the fourth book of the *Aeneid.*)
The imposing man is primarily one who is strong, who can kill a
relatively large number of people. Orlando, Rinaldo, Brandi-
marte, Bradamante, Rodomonte, Ruggiero, Marfisa, Gradasso
and other heroes on both sides in Ariosto are so powerful that
they can easily dismember hundreds of other knights on the
battlefield. Early in the story Rodomonte nearly subdues Paris
and its thousands of defenders single-handed, and any one of the
chief warriors is capable of turning the tide of a general engage-

ment—as, of course, Archilles does in the *Iliad*. The ideal is the
primitive one of quintessential maleness: an ideal still met with in
savage tribes and among teen-age gangs in our own culture. The
"honor" which is valued among such persons is mainly that of
prestige. Any slight is bitterly resented, and especially any impu-
tation of weakness, no matter how indirect. Frustration must be
wiped out by terrible revenge, preferably, but not necessarily,
upon the offending persons. When a fight is impending, the hero
must become terribly angry. His eyes shoot fire, his breast heaves,
he roars at the top of his voice, he quivers with martial impatience. In this mood he can innocently kill, rape, burn, rip to
pieces, or wreak any kind of havoc. In an important aspect, the
ideal is that of the bully-boy; the hero is a dream-fulfillment of
how weaker males might like to be. He lives in a shame culture,
not in a guilt culture. Besides natural honor, there is also a code
of artificial honor which characterizes especially people of the
highest rank, like Charlemagne or, in Tasso, Goffredo. Ruggiero,
although he sometimes breaks solemn vows, also has a relatively
strong sense of artificial honor. In the main, however, honor in
any sense other than prestige plays a minor role. About romantic
love, little need be said except that it often leads heroes into the
abandonment of duty, as it still does in the novels—for instance—of Ian Fleming; but except perhaps in Tasso it has no
idealistic side and implies no unselfish interest in the beloved's
welfare.

That these standards are gone from Milton every undergradu-
ate reader is aware. The English poet is

> Not sedulous by Nature to indite
> Warrs, hitherto the onely Argument
> Heroic deem'd, chief maistrie to dissect
> With long and tedious havoc fabl'd Knights
> In Battels feign'd.
>
> (IX, 27–31)

His preference is for "the better fortitude / Of Patience and Heroic Martyrdom / Unsung" (IX, 31–33). The development of

this higher ideal has been traced by Merritt Hughes in a notable article, and by others after him; but too little attention has been paid, I think, to the recrudescence of the older imperatives in the Renaissance Italians. As for love, in *Paradise Lost* we see something more than the inflaming or melting of the masculine mind by intoxicating beauty. Adam's sin, when it comes, if it is partly egoistic ("How can I live without thee?"—IX, 908), is also partly noble ("from thy State / Mine never shall be parted, bliss or woe"—IX, 915–16). Again we have moved from the instinctual level toward the peculiarly human and spiritual.

The three contrasts I have chosen for emphasis are by no means exhaustive. The substitution of blank verse for the rhymed *ottava rima* of all three Italian poets and the innumerable other rhymed forms attempted by Milton's English predecessors and contemporaries is itself boldly original. Coming to *Paradise Lost* from Renaissance drama, as we now commonly do, we tend to assume, quite wrongly, that Milton picked up an accepted verse form. That he did not do so is clear from a note to the reader in the second edition of 1674: the printer has procured arguments for the separate books, "and withal a reason of that which stumbled many others, why the Poem Rimes not." Instead of adopting unrhymed dramatic verse, Milton deprived epic verse of its rhyme. Again, his poem is "regular"—bound, that is, by the epic rules Aristotle had formulated in his *Poetics*. Milton has excluded secondary plots (unless the fall of the bad angels is thought of as secondary), begun in the middle, restricted the temporal scope, and otherwise imitated what he evidently considered an archetypal model most nearly approximated by Homer and Virgil. Once more, he has created personages whose minds are frequently divided, who are torn by contradictory urges more complicated than the *odi et amo* motif traditional in the portrayal of vacillating lovers; and by doing so he has laid the essential basis for what I have called the vertical depth of his fable. In the Italians, doublemindedness, or indeed even uncertainty, is rare. Still other differences might be noted, many of them important. I hope, however, to have suggested, although in so brief a scope I cannot hope to have proved, that although *Orlando Innamorato, Orlando Furioso,* and *Gerusalemme Liberata* in their own ways are good, and perhaps even the last two "great" poems, *Paradise Lost,* by rejecting their tradition, has attained, even for scientifically oriented minds, a *relevance* which forbids us to discuss it as merely charming.

And this, I submit, is a considerable accomplishment for a poem already three hundred years old.

University of California,
Berkeley, California

NOTES

1. Frank Allen Patterson, general editor, *The Works of John Milton* (New York, 1931–38), Vol. X, 127–28. All future references to Milton's writings will be to this edition.

2. *Ibid.* Vol. III, i, 236–37.

3. I use the London, 1785, edition of Hoole's translation.

4. Torquato Tasso, *La Gerusalemme Liberata* (Milano, 1950).

5. *Poimandres: Studien zur griechisch-aegyptischen und früh-christlichen Literatur* (Leipzig, 1904).

6. Two particularly notable works are the following: A.-J. Festugière, *La Révélation d'Hermès Trismégiste* (Paris, 1949–54), and Walter Scott, *Hermetica* (Oxford, 1924–26).

7. Paul H. Kocher, *Science and Religion in Elizabethan England* (San Marino, California, 1953), p. 202.

8. *Giordano Bruno and the Hermetic Tradition* (London, 1964).

9. Cited *ibid.*, p. 17, from P. O. Kristeller, *Studies in Renaissance Thought and Letters* (Rome, 1956), p. 223 ff., and *Supplementum Ficinianum* (Florence, 1937), pp. lvii–lviii, cxxix–cxxxi.

10. Yates, *op. cit.*, pp. 367–73 and—for the *Picatrix*—p. 54.

11. *Ibid.*, p. 238.

12. "The Divine Pymander of Hermes Trismegistus, Reprinted from the Old English Translation," in *The Journal of Speculative Philosophy,* Vol. XX (July, 1886), 225–27.

THE TRAGIC GLASS:
MILTON, MINTURNO AND
THE *CONDITION HUMAINE*

John M. Steadman

For many critics the prevailing tone of Milton's later poetry is disillusionment.[1] An intrusive pessimism, whose primary causes were biographical and historical, pervades it. Darkened by the premature sunset of the Commonwealth—the untimely twilight of liberty—the works of his major phase border on despair. Taken as a whole, considered ensemble, they form a moving and eloquent expression of personal griefs—blindness, domestic unhappiness, political disappointment, religious isolation. They are (these critics argue) the voice of a poet alienated from his age and conscious rather of its degeneration than of "an age too late." They are the voice of a poet at odds with his society, who can no longer prophesy as its official spokesman, who can no longer champion its values or celebrate its triumphs, who (for his own "conscience and internal peace") can do little more than register a personal protest. They are the voice of a poet who has lost his public authority and can speak only as a private individual. They are a *vox clamantis in deserto;* they sprang out of solitude and spoke to solitude. Unlike the sacred poetry he had envisioned earlier, they were not intended for the theater or the

101

public forum, nor even the church-porch. They were directed to the wilderness, to the Church in the wilderness; they were addressed to a fit audience—and few.

For such critics, *Paradise Lost* and *Samson Agonistes* are essentially private rather than public documents. They are the poet's own *Soliloquies* and *Confessions,* his own spiritual autobiography. He laments the "evil days" on which he has fallen not merely in his own voice but through those of his characters. His epic on Adam's fall and his tragedy of Samson's "victorious agonies" vicariously record his own private and public woes—his loss of sight, his virtual captivity among enemies, his sense of national apostasy.

Anacreon's lyre refused to speak of Atreus and would only hymn the praises of Eros. Milton's heroic trumpet can no longer blazon the alarum to battle or the command to charge. It can only sound a retreat. Or perhaps a dead-march.

Such a view demands respect rather than assent; for, in actuality, the man and the poet are co-existent rather than co-extensive. In its extreme form this attitude substitutes the Crocean conception of art as expression for the Aristotelian (and Miltonic) ideal of art as imitation. Subordinating objective intention to subjective feeling, it eclipses dramatic and narrative modes in an unconscious lyricism. Milton's heroic poetry becomes (it would seem) little more than an expanded complaint, a pretentious variant on the conventional *planctus* or *querela.* Or at best it belongs to a mixed genre, combining the personal elegy with epic and tragedy. In these extended lamentations the poet bewails his own miseries, deplores his countrymen's tragic flaw—or celebrates his own heroic constancy. Universalizing his own distress, he converts his private sorrows into public woes, magnifying England's apostasy into that of humanity and the ruin of the Commonwealth into the downfall of mankind. He elevates his own misfortunes from the level of the particular to that of the universal—the tragedy of the *condition humaine.* The theme of man's greatness and misery, so prominent in his final poems, is actually the "objective correlative" of the poet's own grief.

This is a familiar example of that overemphasis on autobiographical elements in literature to which most scholars are prone and against which they must constantly be on guard. For Professor C. S. Lewis it is the "personal heresy" and for Professor Parker the "autobiographical fallacy."[2] The error lies, of course, not in acknowledging the "personal" and "autobiographical" elements in Milton's verse, but in exaggerating their importance and minimizing other factors of equal or greater significance. However strongly he may have felt his own personal misfortunes and those of his nation, he was well aware that the misery of the human condition had long been a traditional theme of both secular and sacred tragedy and classical as well as Christian philosophy. Against the background of Renaissance poetic theory and Christian doctrine his emphasis on this moral commonplace seems consciously oriented towards literary and theological ends. To this extent his apparent pessimism is a corollary of his choice of literary form and content; it is firmly based on the principles of Renaissance poetics, humanistic ethics and Christian theology.

Of Milton's three major poems, one is a tragedy. The others belong to a narrative genre that Aristotelian poetics had closely associated with tragedy in its choice of persons, its action, and its psychological effects—a genre that had depicted the sufferings of Odysseus, the woes of the Greeks before Troy, the civil wars of Thebes and Rome, and the trials of Job. Is it surprising that an epic like *Paradise Lost*—originally designed as a tragedy— should stress the theme of man's misery? Is it startling that a "tragedy of suffering"[3] like *Samson* should also emphasize man's miserable estate?

Secondly, both humanistic and Christian ethics had extolled the "better fortitude" of patience over the active fortitude exercised in martial combat. Here again Milton's emphasis on suffering is closely linked with his choice of literary genre, with the fact that he is writing heroic poetry. Finally, both Catholic and Protestant traditions had realized the logical and rhetorical force of arguments drawn from the dignity and misery of man. Both had utilized the paradoxes of man's estate, the contradictions of the *condition humaine,* for exhortations to self-knowledge, to repentance, to *contemptus mundi,* to Christian patience and faith, and to the consolations of religion.

The tone of Milton's final poetry is conditioned by poetic genre, by his preference for a heroic ideal centering on patience and martyrdom, and by his theological subject-matter and intent. It is not exclusively, nor even predominately, an expression of subjective feeling.

I

In the first chorus of *Samson Agonistes* Milton adroitly universalizes the personal miseries of the individual hero. From the particular griefs of Samson's "condition" the poet passes to the general instability of the *condition humaine.* Just as the virtues and vices of the protagonist are individual examples of abstract principles that apply, in varying degrees, to all men, so his misfortunes are in a sense indicative, if not emblematic, of those of humanity. The hero's opening speech stresses an individual tragedy; the fallen champion "bemoan(s) his condition" and his personal vulnerability "to all the miseries of life." The Chorus' opening words present, in turn, what is essentially a universal tragedy, emphasizing not merely the lamentable condition of the individual but that of the whole species. After recapitulating the motif of personal woe ("Which shall I first bewail, Thy Bondage or lost Sight"), it shifts the emphasis temporarily to the universal:

O mirror of our fickle state,
Since man on earth unparallel'd!
The rarer thy example stands,
By how much from the top of wondrous glory, . . .
To lowest pitch of abject fortune thou art fall'n.

Samson's fallen condition, like that of Adam in *Paradise Lost,* is the tragic glass in which one may read the miseries of the *conditio hominis,* the universal condition of man.

The central image in this passage is a commonplace—indeed a cliché—but this was rather an asset than a demerit. The very fact that it *was* so conventional actually enhanced its argumentative force. The mirror-metaphor had long been as closely associated with tragedy as with comedy, the proverbial *speculum consuetudinis.* It underlay the catalogue of Fortune's victims in *A Mirror for Magistrates,* and it provided one of the central images in the abdication scene of *Richard II.*

In Minturno's *L'Arte Poetica* Milton could have found this image specifically associated with tragedy as the representation of man's condition and fortune changes. Several critics have stressed the resemblances between Minturno's conception of catharsis and Milton's view,[4] and there is a strong probability that the latter may have read and recalled Minturno's conception of tragedy as a *"lucidissimo specchio"* of the *"umana condizione."*

The office of tragedy, Minturno argues, is to teach, delight, and move ("insegnare, dilettare, muovere"). From the example of Fortune's changes in others, we learn to distrust worldly prosperity and to endure evil with a patient mind. In this way tragedy not only abates the passions, but also teaches the human condition with the mutability of Fortune ("insegni l'umana condizione con la mutazione della Fortuna"). It places before the eyes the example of the life and character of those who surpass all others in greatness, dignity, and fortune, but fall into extreme misery through error. We learn thereby not to trust in worldly things in our prosperity. We learn that all earthly things are frail and subject to death or change. We learn that the greatest may become basest and the happiest the most miserable. Perceiving so great a change of fortune in another's case, we learn that the same may happen in our own. Hence no evil that befalls us will come entirely unexpected. Knowing that our nature is so vulnerable, so obnoxious to evil, we learn to substain it with patience:

Allora intenderete, che cosa sia il fine della
Tragica Poesia, quando avrete inteso, qual sia
l'uficio del Tragico Poeta; il qual non è altro,
che dir talmente in versi, che insegni, e diletti,
e muova sì, che delle passioni abbia a purgare gli
animi de' riguardanti: perciocchè, oltra ch' egli,
sicome ogn' altro Scenico Poeta, si dice insegnare,
quando in Teatro il suo Poema rappresenta; nondimeno
ci reca innanzi agli occhi l'essemplo della vita, e
li costumi espressi di coloro, i quali avanzando
gli altri nelle grandezze, e nelle dignità, e negli
agi della Fortuna, sono per umano errore in estrema
infelicità caduti: acciocchè intendiamo non doverci
nella prosperità delle cose mondane confidare, e niente
esser quaggiù di sì lunga vita, nè sì stabile, che non
sia caduco, e mortale; niente sì felice, che miserabile;
niente sì grande, che basso, e infimo non possa divenire.
E veggendo in altrui tanta mutazion di fortuna, guardarne
sappiamo, che niun male inopinato ci avvenga; e, se
alcun male ci avviene, (Conciò sia che la nostra natura
sottoposta sia tanto al male, ch' egli spesso ci molesta)
sappiamlo con animo paziente sostenere.

Hence, no doctrine or formal instruction can so abate the
passions of the mind as tragedy. It depicts the human condition
as distinctly as in the clearest of mirrors. The beholder perceives
therein the nature of things, the variety and mutability of life,
and the weakness and frailty of man; and he learns thereby to
think of such things without anguish. Instead, in adversity he acts
like a wise man and knows how to console himself in at least
three different ways. First, the thought that he had long ago
anticipated such adversities can prove an excellent remedy to
relieve the mind of its burden of cares. Secondly, he reflects that
it behooves him to bear such human accidents patiently. Thirdly,
he knows that there is no real evil except guilt and that he should

not attribute to guilt those accidental evils which do not proceed
from his own will:

> Laonde è da tenere, niuna dottrina ritrovarsi, che
> tanto abbatta la passione dell' animo, quanto fa
> la Tragica Poesia; conciò sia ch' ella ci rechi
> dinanzi agli occhi non esser cosa, la quale avvenir
> non possa, e chiaramente l'umana condizione ci
> rappresenti in guisa di lucidissimo specchio; nel
> quale chi vede la natura delle cose, e la varietà
> della vita, e la debolezza dell' uomo, non se n'affligge,
> quando queste cose nel penziero si riduce: ma far volendo
> uficio di savio, ne' casi avversi avrà da potersi in
> tre modi consolare. Prima, perchè lungo tempo avrà
> penzato potergli quelle avversità avventire; il qual
> penziero è sopra ogni eccellentissimo rimedio da poter
> la mente di ogni molestia liberare. Dappoi, perchè intende
> gli umani accidenti convenirsi portare. Ultimamente,
> perchè conosce non esser male altro, che la colpa;
> ne doverglisi a colpa attribuire quel, che dalla
> volontà di lui non procede.[5]

Like Milton's preface to Samson, the first Chorus reveals the
seriousness with which he regarded the office of the tragic poet.
In effecting his transition from the level of tragic demonstration
to the level of moral inference—from Samson's condition to the
"fickle state" of mankind—he fulfills two of the three functions
outlined by Minturno. First, he teaches "l'umano condizione con
la mutazione della Fortuna." Secondly, he broadens his appeal to
the passions of pity and fear by emphasizing the point that *all*
men are vulnerable to Fortune's reverses and that Samson's condition is potentially, if not actually, common to us all. Though
the full moral significance and emotional force of this "mirror" of
life's variety and man's weakness ("specchio . . . [della] varietà
della vita, e [della] debolezza dell' uomo") emerge only in the

later development of the plot, they receive their first universal statement and application in this passage.

Though Minturno's requirements are only partially satisfied at this point, they are, for the most part, fulfilled during the subsequent evolution of the fable. The human error (*umano errore*) whereby Samson fell into extreme misery ("in estrema infelicità") is scrupuolously dissected in the scenes with Manoa and Dalila. The dangers of trusting in prosperity and "wordly things" ("cose mondane") are exposed in the condemnation of our "ever failing trust In mortal strength." The necessity of bearing misfortune patiently ("alcun male . . . con animo pazienta") is explicitly stated by the Chorus (lines 652 ff.) and reiterated throughout the drama.

Finally, Milton, like Minturno, lays heavy stress on consolation—the cure or "remedy" of the mind in the midst of misery. For both, this is an essential part of the therapeutic and cathartic role of tragedy; and it is significant that both *Samson Agonistes* and *Paradise Lost* conclude on this note. Michael's message to fallen mankind is not merely an admonition but a *consolatio*. Enjoined to "dismiss them not disconsolate," he leaves Adam "greatly satisfied and recomforted" and Eve herself "compos'd to quietness of mind and submission." Adam departs "Greatly instructed, . . . Greatly in peace of thought." The Chorus in *Samson* departs with similar tranquillity of mind. It too is "dismist" with "peace and consolation . . . , And calm of mind, all passion spent."

This is the Christian equivalent of the Stoic *consolatio*. Like the latter, it attempts to comfort; like the latter, it seeks to moderate the passions and restore tranquillity of mind. Nevertheless in spirit and doctrine it is radically different—as different as Adam's quiet of mind from Stoic apathy, as Christian patience from its Stoic counterpart—or, indeed, as Christian and Stoic Providence.[6] Though Christian and Stoic alike regarded submission to Providence as a primary source of consolation, they differed profoundly in their conceptions of Providence and in their attitudes towards it. Though both acknowledged the Logos, the Supernal Wisdom, as the supreme governor of the universe, the Christian possessed in Scripture a partial manifestation of the providential design, a veiled but valid revelation of its "inscrutable intent." Unlike the Stoic, he possessed a divine *promise;* and, in all three of Milton's final poems, this serves both as an object of faith and as a means of consolation. Unlike the Stoic, the Christian possessed a hope, an *expectation.* To the cardinal virtues of fortitude and wisdom he could add at least two of the theological virtues.

There was, moreover, a second difference equally fundamental. The classical Stoic could find consolation in his own rectitude; his own "conscious virtue" made him superior to whatever indignities Fortune heaped upon him. The Christian, on the other hand, had to reckon with a sense of his own unworthiness, the inescapable fact of his own sin. For consolation he could turn less to his own intrinsic virtue (though the Christian Stoics of the Renaissance sometimes did so) than to his belief in divine mercy and to the ministrations of the Spirit itself, the Comforter.

Hence in all three poems we find Milton drawing a sharp distinction between Stoic and Christian modes of consolation. In *Paradise Regain'd* he accuses the Stoic of "Philosophic pride." In *Paradise Lost* he portrays the fallen angels discoursing on Stoic commonplaces—Providence and Foreknowledge, Will and Fate, Passion and Apathy—and arming their "obdured heart[s] with stubborn patience." In *Samson Agonistes* he stresses the inadequacy of "Consolatories writ With studied argument and much persuasion" without "Some source of consolation from above," without the "secret refreshings" infused by the Spirit. Like his righteousness the Christian must seek his consolation less from himself than from Heaven. On this point the Christian *consolatio* is worlds apart from the classical.

Milton's *consolatio,* in turn, differs most markedly from Minturno's precisely where it diverges most strikingly from that of the Stoic—in the sense of guilt. The knowledge that true misery is guilt ("non esser male altro, che la colpa") can bring no comfort to Samson. On the contrary, for him, as for Adam, the recognition of his guilt and the knowledge of his sin merely exacerbate his grief. As both perceive and acknowledge, sin is essential misery.

II

> God of our Fathers, what is man!
> That thou towards him with hand so various,
> Or might I say contrarious,
> Temperst thy providence through his short course . . .
> Just or unjust, alike seem miserable,
> For oft alike, both come to evil end.

These lines are rather a complaint to Providence than a protest against it. They question, rather than challenge, the ways of God to men. But the issue that they raise is not merely a rhetorical question. It involves, in fact, one of the central problems of *Samson Agonistes* and *Paradise Lost*—the wisdom and justice of God's government of man. Despite their differences in form, argument, and genre, this is a question that both poems attempt to answer, and their answer is not only explicit in the final utterances of the principal speakers, but implicit in the complication and solution of the plot or fable.

The same passage also voices another theological commonplace—the misery of the *condition humaine*. Here, however, there is a concealed ambiguity or equivoque, for the misery of the just and the unjust is not the same. It only "seems" to be.

At this point the Chorus appropriately dwells on the misery rather than the dignity of man. Yet the one complements the other, and in most theological discussions of these topics they are inseparable. The opening line of this choral ode echoes the Eighth Psalm, where the query "what is man" is clearly associated with man's native dignity. (The Authorized Version explicitly links it with "God's love to man.") In associating this passage with the misery of man's estate, Milton has placed it in an altogether different context, where its full significance necessarily appears incomplete. He has intentionally presented it as a half-truth, whose full meaning is apparent only in terms of its original context: "What is man, that thou art mindful of him? and the son of man, that thou visitest him? Thou madest him to have dominion over the works of thy hands; thou hast put all things under his feet." Nor is the meaning really complete apart from the glorification of God's name, with which the psalm begins and ends: "O Lord our Lord, how excellent is thy name in all the earth!"[7]

The dignity and misery of man were, in fact, as closely "involved and interwoven" as good and evil seemed to Milton. If they did not actually spring "from out the rind of one apple tasted," they were nevertheless as inseparable as "two twins cleaving together." They testified to a certain monstrous and unnatural deformity in the very nature of man, a cogential flaw apparent from his birth. The paradoxes of his character and the contradictions of his condition intrigued Western poets from Sophocles to Pope, and for several writers (Robert Burton, for instance) they held the same morbid fascination as Siamese twins.

In Milton's treatment of the dignity and misery of man—we can distinguish two primary emphases; the one predominately tragic, the other potentially heroic. The first stressed man's responsibility for his own misery. The second emphasized the positive value of adversity as the means and occasion of testing and manifesting the hero's patience and faith. Both provided a basis for a theodicy and a psychology; both helped to "justify" the ways of God and to stimulate man's inquiry into his own nature and condition. Both increased his limited understanding of Providence and his knowledge of himself.

If the first is most prominent in *Paradise Lost,* the latter was (for many of Milton's contemporaries) especially marked in the Book of Job. Both, in turn, underlie the spiritual dialectics of *Samson Agonistes.* Milton's drama has always resisted the clear-cut, but oversimplified formulas that critics have tried to foist upon it. The reason lies partly in the complexity of Samson's predicament, and the human predicament it epitomizes. The causes and significance of his sufferings are not simple and univocal, but varied, complex and polysemous. The evils he endures are punishment for his own transgression; as he himself confesses, he has brought them on himself. Nevertheless he does endure them; and they become, accordingly, the matter of heroic virtue. They exercise and "illustrate" his patience and faith. Finally, they provide the occasion for his greatest triumph—the victory that Jehovah's Providence had, all along, been preparing for him, "The work to which [he] was divinely call'd."

The focus of the tragic vision has normally centered on the human condition; the tragic plot has usually hinged on the paradox of man's dignity and misery. Milton's chief innovation on this facet of the epic and tragic tradition was to assimilate it to theological tradition and thus convert the ordeal of the tragic hero into an instrument of self-knowledge.[8] The spiritual struggles which Samson and Adam alike undergo after their fall follow a pattern clearly defined by both Catholic and Protestant theologians. Though expressed in various terms, the pattern itself remains relatively uniform. Beginning with a consideration of man's original dignity and present misery, it contrasts his native condition with his fallen estate. Drawing a sharp distinction between the misery of sin and the misery of punishment and deducing both from Adam's fall, it proceeds logically to the remedy —the ultimate release from misery through the merits of Christ and the ministrations of the Spirit and / or the Church. A Ramist theologian,[9] whose works Milton knew, expresses this pattern in terms of the dichotomy of Christian "pathology" and "therapeutics," the one concerned with "the misery of man's condition" and the other with its remedy. One can, with some degree of probability, read this dichotomy into *Samson* and the latter books of *Paradise Lost,* but it is scarcely necessary to do so. The essential features of this pattern are common to numerous theologians, and on this point at least it seems preferable to consider Milton's treatment of the *condition humaine* in relation to the tradition as a whole rather than to a single author.

The "vision of tragedy," as Professor Sewall reminds us, is frequently a "double vision"; the "tragic glass" is, in a very real sense, bifocal. Beyond the limits of human vision—blinded by passion and tears, shadowed by doubts, and darkened by its own mortality—there is the Providential view, the eternal vision that "sees all things at one view." Above the clash and contradictions of human wills, there is one inscrutable and irresistible purpose, one ineluctable and "uncontrollable intent." To Christian tragedy it is axiomatic that this divine perspective should be alien to the *condition humaine;* and, in the tragic hero's progressive insight into his own situation and the general condition of man, it is equally imperative that he should recognize this fact, should acknowledge the limitations of his own vision. Thus Samson, Manoa, and the Chorus tend (like Job) to doubt, question, challenge, and lament "the ways of God" and the "method" of His justice; but they also continue (like Job) to "trust in Him."

Like Job, Milton's protagonist is a hero of faith, whose patience and constancy are tried and perfected in suffering. In this context one recalls Sewall's quotation from Kierkegaard: "even the most tried of the tragic heroes walks with dancing step compared with the knight of faith." For "the knight of faith is kept in constant tension"—"kept sleepless, for he is constantly tried."[10]

If tragedy is indeed what Milton believed it to be—"the gravest, moralest, and most profitable of all other Poems"—its claim to so lofty a title rests largely on its universality. Its portrait of an individual *agon* mirrors the accumulated agony of a race. The "tragic glass" casts back to us the image of ourselves, and in the ordeal of Samson or Oedipus we read the *condition humaine.* (Both heroes learn, in fact, that for all their heroic eminence, their fame as saviors and deliverers of their peoples, they are not exempt from the common lot and from the vicissitudes and frailty of mankind.) Thus the tragic hero becomes an emblem of (and, at his highest, a surrogate for) humanity. In universalizing Samson's predicament into a "mirror of our fickle state," Milton bears eloquent witness to the gravity and universality of the tragic vision.

The Huntington Library

NOTES

1. Cf. E. M. W. Tillyard, "Milton and the English Epic Tradition," in *Seventeenth Century Studies Presented to Sir Herbert Grierson* (Oxford, 1938) pp. 211–234; J. B. Broadbent, *Some Graver Subject: An Essay on Paradise Lost* (London, 1960); W. Menzies, *"Milton: The Last Poems,"* *Essays and Studies*, Vol. XXIV (1938), pp. 80–113; for summaries of the views of Visiak, Kreipe, and others, see the discussion by Merritt Y. Hughes in *John Milton, Complete Poems* (New York, 1957), pp. 531–548.

2. Cf. E. M. W. Tillyard and C. S. Lewis, *The Personal Heresy, A Controversy* (London, 1939) and William R. Parker, "The Date of *Samson Agonistes*," *Philiological Quarterly*, Vol. XXVIII (1945), pp. 145–166.

3. See Aristotle, *On the Art of Poetry*, trans. Ingram Bywater (Oxford, 1909), p. 53; Parker, *Milton's Debt to Greek Tragedy in Samson Agonistes* (Baltimore, 1937).

4. See J. E. Spingarn, *A History of Literary Criticism in the Renaissance* (New York, 1899), pp. 79–81; Ida F. Langdon, *Milton's Theory of Poetry and Fine Art* (New York, 1924), *passim*.

5. *L'Arte Poetica del Signor Antonio Minturno* (Napoli, 1725), pp. 76–77.

6. Among the primary topics of the stoic *consolatio* are the justice, benevolence, and reasonableness of Providence, the good of the whole universe, the freedom of the individual will, and submission to the will of God or Nature. Cf. *The Stoic and Epicurean Philosophers*, ed. Whitney J. Oates (New York, 1940), pp. 370, 390, 414–5, 468, 474–6, 497, and *passim*.

7. With the Psalmist's query we must couple "the existential question" (as Professor Sewall terms it) in Job vii. 17–18 and XV. 14. On Job's lips it is a complaint against Providence: "What is man, that thou shouldest magnify him? And that thou shouldest set thine heart upon him? And that thou shouldest visit him every morning, and try him every moment?" In

Eliphaz's mouth it is a rebuke to Job for attempting to justify himself: "What is man, that he should be clean? And he which is born of a woman, that he should be righteous?" Hebrews ii. 6–7 interprets the words of the Eighth Psalm (Authorized Version) as a prophecy of Christ. In Psalm CXLIV. 3–4 the immediate context of a similar query ("Lord, what is man, that thou takest knowledge of him! or the son of man, that thou makest account of him! Man is like to vanity: his days are as a shadow that passeth away") is the Psalmist's expression of "trust" in God as his "strength" and "fortress," his "high tower" and his "deliverer." With the possible exception of the passage in Hebrews, all of these texts are clearly relevant to the Chorus' query in *Samson Agonistes*. Like Job it raises the issues of the sufferings of the just and the apparently "unequal" and "contradictory" ways of God with men. Like Job (and like *Paradise Lost*) Milton's drama is essentially a theodicy. Like the Book of Job, it questions man's nature and God's Providence only to provide a stronger and more forceful answer "in the close"—an answer, provided by divine testimony itself, that resolves the tension between man's suffering and God's design, vindicates supernal justice, and allays doubts by a valid confirmation of faith. The context of the 144th Psalm is equally relevant; Milton's protagonist is a "hero of faith" who accomplishes "God's propos'd deliverance" not so much through his own might as through a strength divinely given. (For "the existential question," see Richard B. Sewall, *The Vision of Tragedy* (New Haven and London, 1965), pp. 5, 18).

8. For the theme of self-knowledge in Milton's poetry, see Arnold Stein, *Heroic Knowledge: An Interpretation of Paradise Regained and Samson Agonistes* (Minneapolis, 1957).

9. Cf. Bartholomew Keckermann, *Systema SS. Theologiae*. For Milton and Ramism, see Wilbur Samuel Howell, *Logic and Rhetoric in England, 1500–1700* (Princeton, 1956); Walter J. Ong, S. J., *Ramus, Method, and the Decay of Dialogue* (Cambridge, Mass., 1958); and Leon Howard, "The Invention of Milton's Great Argument: A Study of the Logic of God's Ways to Men," *Huntington Library Quarterly*, Vol. IX (1946), pp. 149–173.

10. Sewall, p. 52.

MILTON AND THE HUNDRED ARTICLES AGAINST ALEXANDER MORE

by Kester Svendsen

This is a paper read at the annual meeting of the Milton Society of America, MLA Convention, December, 1966.

After nearly three centuries in a Charenton cemetery, the unquiet dust of Alexander More is once again disturbed by echoes of his catastrophic encounter with Milton. Recent scholarship has resurrected More's memory along with that of *Pro Se Defensio,* the second of the poet's sulphurous attacks upon the supposed author of *Regii Sanguinis Clamor.* That anonymous castigation of Milton and the Commonwealth had actually been composed by Peter du Moulin the Younger; but it had been seen through the Hague press of Adrian Vlacq by More in 1652, and it was immediately attributed to him by Continental gossip. Milton replied in 1654 with *Defensio Secunda,* in which he identified Alexander More as the author and systematically dismembered his character and reputation. More asserted his innocence in *Fides Publica* (1654–55); and Milton, embarrassed but undaunted, had the last sanguinary word in the *Pro Se Defensio* of 1655, an awesome document in the rhetoric of character-acter assassination.[1]

A remarkable feature of this work is the accuracy of Milton's information on nearly every question except the central one of authorship. In order to fasten legal if not auctorial responsibility upon More and to obscure his own blunder, Milton exploited every available polemic device and discreditable rumor in reviewing the testimonials adduced by More and in rehearsing sordid details of the scandalous career of his last major antagonist. Many of his charges are corroborated by the minute books or *Registers* of the Petty Council of Geneva and of the Venerable Company of Pastors and Professors of the Academy of Geneva for 1639–1649, as well as by other Geneva documents. Milton alludes to so many particulars embodied in these archives that his indirect access to them is indisputable. More was the focus of a power struggle between civil and ecclesiastical authorities; his enemies in Geneva happily furnished Milton with details of the conflict. Chief among many issues between More and the Company of Pastors were the "hundred articles" concerning More's doctrine and deportment filed against him in 1648–49. These are mentioned repeatedly in *Council* and *Company Registers;* they are preserved in *Archives Tronchin* and in MS 468 *Affaire Alexandre Morus,* a collection assembled by Thomas Claparède and Auguste Bouvier. Their content was communicated to Milton, it now seems clear, by François Turretin, a member of the Company of Pastors in 1648–49 and brother to a London acquaintance of Milton. The present study deals more intensively with the hundred articles and their implications than space permitted in the earlier notice of them. The matter is of some importance to our understanding of Milton's style because he used information about More as he used classical mythology and biblical geography in his poetry—a body of knowledge out of which he could fashion an allusive and persuasive discourse. And the articles themselves offer an illuminating insight into the theological controversy that eventually destroyed Calvinism.[2]

While *Defensio Secunda* was in preparation and in press, Milton had been told by Samuel Hartlib and others that More was not the author of *Regii Sanguinis Clamor;* but he refused to withdraw the book because, as he put it, all denials had originated with More himself and were therefore of no account. However shaky this explanation may seem to a modern reader and however untenable Milton's position actually was, he began at once to collect additional ammunition bearing on More's responsibility and on his disreputable career as evidenced in conflicts with the Company of Pastors. Long before 1655 Milton had effected communication with Geneva. In March of that year he wrote Ezekiel Spanheim, son of More's enemy Frederick, thanking him for information usable in *Pro Se Defensio,* and concluding: "Meanwhile you can, I think, without hesitation address any letters you write me to Turretin of Geneva, now staying in London, whose brother over there you know; through whom, as this of mine will reach you most conveniently, so yours will come to me." This brother was François Turretin, whose family had been identified with Geneva for nearly a century. He arrived late upon the scene of More's disputes with the Company; but apparently at once made bond with Theodore Tronchin, Jean François Mermilliod, and André Pictet as pastors unalterably opposed to More. *Company Registers* show his attendance at meetings about the hundred articles. The inescapable conclusion, in view of Milton's letter to Spanheim, is that he passed on to Milton by way of his brother the details of More's struggles with Council and Company.[3]

The hundred articles overtook Alexander More in 1648. He was a liberal Calvinist influenced by the Saumurian movement toward universal grace, unlimited atonement, and other heresies. He came to Geneva in 1639, won a professorship of Greek in public competition at age twenty-three and seemed destined for a brilliant career, despite an already ominous disinclination to mortify the flesh. But early he fell foul of conservatives like Tronchin and Pictet, the latter a relative of Frederick Spanheim. His certification to the Geneva ministry was delayed from June to October 1641 while the Company challenged his qualifications;

and only upon pressure from the Petty Council was he admitted
to the pulpit in late January 1642. Even at this time, when he
was barely twenty-six years old, rumors about his exploits as a
voluptuary accompanied those about his irregularities in doctrine. He rode out all storms and actually obtained Company
recommendation to the post of Rector of the Academy September 12, 1645, and Council approval ten days later. But these
marriage meats presaged a funeral table. On January 2, 1646
the Company ordered More to submit his lecture notes for their
review; and once again he was saved from censure only by a
Council intervention which cleared him in presence of the Company January 21, 1646.

Yet word of these difficulties had sifted abroad; and on April
21, 1646 More requested the Council to order an attestation of
his clearance which might be sent into the Low Countries to
counteract unfavorable gossip there. He got it, and matters
rocked along until he published on October 20 an oration on
peace at which Frederick Spanheim, then in Leyden, took offense. By late January 1648, More was up to his ears in trouble,
for the Company refused to certify him to the church of Lyons
(which had invited him to its pastorate) and was resisting Council pressure to issue a confirmation of the previous attestation. On
May 9, 1648 Middelburg, inspired by Salmasius, also asked for
More. Dozens of exchanges between Council and Company over
More's doctrine culminated in the Council's issue, July 28,
1648, of a three-months leave of absence during which More
might go to Middelburg and clear himself. Strong representations
from the Company (which had denied More's request on the
same day) forced an about-face; and the Council appointed a
committee to dissuade More from the trip with the promise of a
glowing testimonial to be sent Middelburg. Jean Diodati persuaded him to stay, but More insisted upon a similarly commend-
atory letter from the Company; and the fat was in the fire. The
Council wanted everything smoothed over so that More could
depart in peace; but after issuing a guarded testimonial, the

Company refused to compromise its principles further by enthusiastic endorsement of a man who would disgrace the Church and the Academy.[4]

On August 15, 1648 the Company decided to interrogate More on charges of heresy and misconduct formulated from those at issue in 1641 and 1646 as well as from More's subsequent career. These became the hundred articles Milton refers to in *Defensio Secunda* and *Pro Se Defensio* as sealed up in the public library. More complained to the Council about the *"cent ou six vingts articles"* on September 27; and a month later, while the Company was delaying action, the Council converted his leave to outright release and ordered the Company to provide appropriate testimonials. That body refused on the grounds that decision had been taken out of their hands, that More was by reason of his release no longer one of them, and that in any case a full-scale examination of More's doctrine and deportment would be necessary before a testimonial could be written. Much wrangling ensued between Council and Company over the content and wording of charges and questions, with More working both sides of the street to exclude awkward queries about his theology and his (for a cleric) spectacular venery. The Company wanted him to reply *"simplement et purement";* he insisted upon annotating each answer. The Church of Middelburg, alarmed by the circulation of testimonials and counter testimonials in the Low Countries, addressed several anxious appeals to Council and Company for clarification and for unqualified endorsement. January and February of 1649 were crowded with meetings over the matter. At last, after six months of turbulence, heartburn, joint committees of review, and parliamentary evasions, a compromise was reached and More, having signed everything required, departed a day or two after July 2, 1649 for Middelburg, Salmasius, and the appointment in Samarra his reputation was to keep with Milton. But the hundred articles stayed behind.[5]

These had been developed in 1647–48 by the Company, leaked to the Low Countries, forwarded by Middelburg to More for his reply, and then used by the Company as the basis of its examination of More in 1648–49. They exist in two known copies, one in MS 468 *Affaire Alexandre Morus,* one in *Archives Tronchin;* a third, given More at Council order, has not turned up. Milton refers to them first in *Defensio Secunda* as "still kept in the public library of Geneva," returns to the charge in *Pro Se Defensio* in sardonic allusion to a volume of More's "works," and later describes More's acts as "already public, stored up in the library of Geneva to the number of well-nigh a hundred articles," of which "those who at that time were involved in all that business in Geneva . . . still do speak." The most violent uproar over them occurred when the Company, deciding at last to collate another copy for the Council, added the damning statement *"que le ministere dudit Sr. Morus ne peut estre en edification en ceste Eglise et Academie."* Certainly the chief points in them add up to some justification for that view.[6]

The articles concern More's unprofessional conduct, his heterodoxy as exhibited in writings and lecture notes, and his scandalous behavior. The format in which they finally were transmitted to the Council and sealed up in the library featured, section by section, a charge by the Company, a reply by More, and a counter-comment by the Company. The first thirty-one articles range in gravity from More's angling for a job elsewhere and his slander of colleagues to his blasphemy and heresy; some must seem hilariously irrelevant today. A selection will indicate how relentlessly the Company attacked their agile antagonist and how closely many of Milton's assertions parallel sections of the indictment.

Art. 1.   Q'uil a envoyé le Sr. Gros au Pays bas avec lettres pour obtenir une Eglise en ce pays la. A respondu qu'il n'a point envoyé ledit Gros: mais que partant et que ses affaires le portoient au lieu ou l'on s'embarque pour aller en Holland, il pourra prendre le dessein de l'aller voir, et en ce cas luy demandoit lettres da recommendation. Il luy en bailla deux qui ne contenoyent que recommendation, et depuis ayant sçie qu'il y estoit, ne luy a donné aucune commission que ne soit très-digne d'un homme de bien. Surquoy la Compagnie a dit 1°. Qu'il suppose contre verité que ledit Gros fust incertain de faire le voyage, puis qu'il luy a baillé les lettres de la Seigneurie, addressantes à l' Eglise de Migdelbourg. 2°. Qu'il a juré et rejuré les affaires de Mr. Morus, l'a recommandé aux principaux de l'Eglise. 3°. Que M. Morus a fait courir le bruit que ledit Gros avoit esté arresté à Paris. Pour preuve de ce que [dessus] faudra voir les lettres de M. Spanheim, et [iusquas] à ce dernier le present article. . . .[7]

Art. 6. Qu'il a demandé advis à la Compagnie, s'il devoit demander congé, le quel il avoit desia demandé à Messieurs. A respondu qu'il avoit desia respondu à cela et qu'il n'avoit pas demandé Conseil s'il demanderoit congé: mais seulement comment il avoit à se conduire, l'ayant obtenu, et qu'il prioit la Compagnie de l'excuser, si à cause de la briefeté du temps il l'avoit demandé à Messieurs en mesme temps. A esté dit par la Compagnie, que veritablement il luy avoit demande [conseil] s'il demanderoit congé à Messieurs ausquels il l'avoit desia demandé, que cela est une moquerie contre la Compagnie, et une menterie en le desquisant et niant. . . .[8]

Art. 9. Qu'il a recherché des Eglises estrangères. A respondu 1°. Qu'il estoit homme de bien. 2°. Qu'il nioit le contenu aus [ledit] article. A esté justifié 1°. Par une lettre de M. de Saulmaise, qu'il l'avoit sollicité de luy trouver une place en Hollande. 2°. A esté sousteau qu'il avoit recherché l'Eglise de Lyon. . . .[9]

Art. 17. Qu'il a reçue des lettres de M. Hotton addressées à la Compagnie qu'il a ouverte sans authorité de celle, n'estant point Moderateur, et les a gardé 3 sepmaines avant que les rendre. A respondu qu'il avoit desia respondu quy devant, sçavoir qu'il avoit reçue un livre par les mains de M. Calendrin avec une lettre, estimant que ce fist une affaire Rectorale, il l'avoit ouverte, et la fit voir à la Compagnie, non pas à la première seance, ou il ne se rencontra pas, mais à la suivante. La Compagnie a iugé comment sur la precedent article. . . .[10]

Art. 26. Il a dit en Consistoire que l'Arrest de Messieurs contre l'Élu estoit iniuste et qu'il le seroit bien romper. L'a advoué: mais qu'il avoit peu dire. . . .[11]

Art. 29. En expliquant le texte de la Magdeleine, il a employé une partie de l'heure à descrire les attraicts d'une putain. A dit qu'il avoit descript ceste pecheusse, comme une vilaine putain, ayant tiré les termes des anciens avec grand choix, et triage.[12]

Art. 30. Qu'il porte des livres profanes au Temple, et notamment Ovide. L'a advoué, mais que cela est arrivé par surprise, ayant pris l'Ovide qui estoit de mesme pareure avec un Testament qui estoit au logis, et qu'il n'estoit pas à luy, a néantmoins nié que cela luy fut arrivé d'autres fois.[13]

Articles touchant la doctrine. . . .

Art. 2. Qu'il favorise la Doctrine de Saumur en sa Harangue de Pace. A respondu que la Harangue de Pace est une chose iugée, ayant esté examinée par trois Syndics Deputés et trois Professeurs en Theologie, Mons. Le Syndicq Pictet la contestant. Ouïes ses responses, a esté dit que sa harangue seroit publiée. La Compagnie a dit 1°. Que la harangue a esté publiée avant la tenue de la Commission. 2°. Qu'en ladit Commission l'on avoit traicté seulement le faict particulier de MM. Pictet et Spanheim, ainsi qu'on a reporté MM. Tronchin et Leger. . . .[14]

Art 5. Qu'il respondu sur l'accusation qu'a fait le Sr. Bernins contre luy touchant la Divinité du St. Esprit, et s'il n'avoit iamais donné occasion à ladit accusation. A respon-

du ne sçavoir qu'elle occasion a en le Sr. Bernins, que est
une pure calomnie, qu'il n's iamais parlé en particulier de
ceste matière avec luy. La Compagnie a dit que s' agissant
d'une question de faict, elle n'en pouvoit decider, et laissoit
ledit Sr. Morus au iugement de Dieu et de sa con-
sçience. . . .[15]

Articles tirés des Dictats de M. Morus

Le Registre de la V. C. fait foy que quand M. Morus fut
reçu au St. Ministre, il promit de n'enseigner, ni en public, ni
en particulier aucune Doctrine contraire, ni diverse d'avec
celle qui a esté icy proposée, ni en aucune nouvelle meth-
ode, et qu'en cas qu'il y [controvisme] il se submettoit à
tout ce qu'il plairoit à la Compagnie d'ordonner de luy, il
signa telles promesses avec les questions et responses.
Néantmoins il a contrevenu en ce qu'on la demande. . . .[16]

The final page of the hundred articles contains, without title or
preamble two charges based on scandalous association with
women.

A esté encor proposé que ledit More s'est trouvé desguisé
en une Compagnie, et avoit de nuict esté voir une Damoi-
selle au pays de Vaud dont a esté donné suiect de Scandale.
Item qu'il a en trop grandes familiarités avec Nicolarde
Pelet tant dans son logis, que dans un Jardin à plein Palais
au grand Scandale de plusieurs personnes.[17]

The repercussions of the hundred articles were to trouble Geneva for many years. More's heretical opinions became the classical issues between conservative and liberal Calvinism. As the
pendulum swung toward Montauban and Saumur in the 1660s,
the Council not uncharacteristically required all pastors to sign
the orthodox profession of faith abstracted from these same articles. To Alexander More, unconcerned about the future of Geneva and fighting for his own ecclesiastical hide, they were a
tightrope nightmare. He tried to conciliate every indictment of
his doctrine, for he wanted clearance. Apparently as a point of

honor, he kept qualifying and annotating his responses; his tongue dropped manna, but without making the worse appear the better reason. By some gentlemen's agreement he seems never to have been required to deal directly with what he and the Council most feared: his amours with the woman of Vaud and with Nicolarde Pelet. These unsavory matters were, however, the particulars most useful to Milton in discrediting his hapless opponent. He alluded to the heresies but did not press the point, partly no doubt because they lacked the sensationalism of More's private life but partly because he concurred in some of their tenets.

In a general sense, then, the charges dramatize a great schism in Calvinism. In a narrower sense, as they enumerate the chief discontents between the brilliant young preacher and his indefatigable enemies, they delineate an undiplomatic but articulate and tough-minded churchman. Except for his impatience with his elders and his fatal gallantry, his career at Geneva and elsewhere might have provided the substance of a tragedy instead of the melodrama it became. Finally, in a special sense the charges illuminate a great poet's assault upon an antagonist both personal and public; for the hundred articles against Alexander More provided Milton exactly what he needed to obscure his own error in attributing *Regii Sanguinis Clamor* to that belated son of Belial.

University of Oregon

NOTES

1. After Masson and Alfred Stern, *Milton and sein Zeit* (2 vols. Leipzig, 1877–79), the most extensive accounts of the Milton-More controversy are J. Milton French, *The Life Records of John Milton* (5 vols. New Brunswick, 1949–1958); Kester Svendsen, "Milton's *Pro Se Defensio* and Alexander More," University of Texas *Studies in Literature and Language*, I, (1959), 11–29, and "Milton and Alexander More: New Documents," *JEGP*, LX (1961), 796–807; and Don M. Wolfe ed., *Complete Prose Works of John Milton* (8 vols. New Haven, 1953-), IV (1966), 274–283, 687–825. My interpretation of the evidence differs in

some respects from those of Wolfe and of Donald Roberts, whose edition of *Defensio Secunda* precedes mine of *Pro Se Defensio* in the volume; but we agree on most of the facts.

2. The provenance of these MSS and others, such as the letters of Salmasius and Elizabeth of Bohemia, is discussed in *Complete Prose*, IV, 689 n. This material has been obtained through the courtesy of Dr. Peter Wegelin of Berne, M. Louis Binz, associate archivist, and M. Bernard Gagnebin, curator of MSS, of Bibliothéque Publique et Universitaire de Genéve. Altogether the new documents amount to more than a thousand pages, many of them deciphered only with the paleographic skill and patience of my research assistant, Mrs. Irene C. Bradley. Some of the correspondences between these archives and Milton's charges are set forth in the annotations to *Pro Se Defensio* in *Complete Prose*, IV, 687–825. The present review of evidence extends these to the hundred articles.

3. See *Complete Prose*, IV, 702 n, for a review of the probable state of Milton's knowledge. Du Moulin, in his *Poemata Libelli Tres* (Cambridge, 1670), pp. 141–42, published fifteen years after the event, alleges: *"At Morus, tantae invidiae impar, in Regia causa frigere coepit,* & Clamorem *Authorem* Miltono *indicavit"* (French, *Life Records*, V, 20). Liljegren and Saurat of course believe that Milton was completely unscrupulous in maintaining More's guilt. Masson, who knew more about the matter than anyone else, does not. Milton's Genevan correspondents have been variously attested. Charles Borgeaud, *Histoire de l' Université de Genève: L'Academie de Calvin* (Geneva, 1900), p. 356 n, declares: "Les relations que le poète puritain avait conservées avec les genevois, depuis son passage à genève, lui permirent d' y poursuivre une enquète. Il eut connaissance des soupçons aux quels avait donné lieu la conduite privée de son antagoniste. . . ." Borgeaud gives a portrait of François Turretin (p. 402) and notes his elevation to the rectorate in 1654, following Philip Mestrezat, who followed More in 1649. French, IV, 19–21, prints the full text of the letter to Spanheim. In *Pro Se Defensio* Milton names Theodore Tronchin (1582–1657), Jean François Mermilliod (1613–1652), and André Pictet (fl. 1640–1650) as More's chief accusers (*Complete Prose*, IV, 798). These three (who never did sign More's testimonials) and François Turretin were present at many weekly meetings of the Company in 1648–1649. Documentary evidence is only partial because of inconsistent secretarial practice. Sometimes the scribes named all pastors and professors in attendance; sometimes they listed only two or three names and the addition *et tous* when all members were present. In the extracts available to me Tronchin attended nearly all the one hundred sessions devoted to More from July 19, 1639, when More was considered for the professorship of Greek, to July 2, 1649, when he was at last given clearance papers (*Company Registers*, No. 8, p. 379; No. 9, p. 232). Mermilliod and Pictet are specifically recorded as attending about thirty times during the same period, though doubtless they are included in the *et*

tous of many entries. François Turretin (1623–1687), who was admitted
to the ministry in 1648, first appears in these papers at the meeting of 15
August 1648, when Mermilliod, Pictet, and Tronchin were also on hand
(*Company Registers,* No. 9, p. 179). Bayle reports a eulogy of François
Turretin by a cousin named Pictet who is possibly the one mentioned by
Milton (*A General Dictionary* [London, 1734], IX, 653). On several
occasions More tried in vain to have Tronchin, Mermilliod, and Pictet
excluded from judging his case (*Company Registers,* No. 9, p. 176).

4. *Company Registers,* No. 8, p. 382, for 2 August 1639 records selection of More for the professorship. On the other data given above, see pp.
432–35; No. 9, p. 84, 92, 156, 176, 189, 207–208; and *Council Registers,*
No. 145, p. 33, 143–144; No. 146, f. 154v, p. 313.

5. *Company Registers,* No. 9, pp. 179, 186–87. Elizabeth of Bohemia
wrote on August 10, 1648; the letter survives in *Archives de Genève* MS
3191, but apparently it was not answered until June 15, 1649, when the
Council approved dispatch of letters to her, to Salmasius, and to More's
father (*Council Registers,* No. 147, pp. 369–70, 379; No. 148, pp.
313–17, 343–49). The articles remained in the library as protection to the
Company against More's changing his tune once clear of Geneva (*Company Registers,* No. 9, p. 192).

6. The original seems to have disappeared. My note, *Complete Prose,*
IV, 753, incorrectly identifies the MS468 copy as the original. As the one
sealed up in the library, it should be the original from which the Company
on January 19, 1649, ordered two copies made, collated, and signed by
the moderator Jacques Sartoris and the secretary De La Fontaine (*Company Registers,* No. 9, p. 201); but it is described as a copy by the
signatories. It runs to twenty-four pages. The copy in *Archives Tronchin,*
which includes a cover sheet with an explanatory note by More, also
comprises twenty-four pages, but in a different hand; it is attested by the
same Company officers. Milton's references are at *Complete Prose,* IV,
567, 753, 779, 787. The Company minutes for February 16, 1648, report
its damaging addition to the articles (*Company Registers,* No. 9, p. 208).
This extract appears in MS468 as well as in *Archives Tronchin.*

7. MS468, p. 1. The almost indecipherable text of this MS has been
collated with the copy in *Archives Tronchin;* doubtful readings are bracketed. Except for expanding a few contracted forms like *le dit, pour,* and
-ment, I have transcribed the Genevan documents literally, with no
attempt to regularize spelling, punctuation, or diacritical marking. The
scribes were not always elegant nor even grammatical or consistent. With
reference to this first article, it should be noted that Milton hammered at
More's repeated attempts to find a pastorate in the Netherlands and
France. See *Complete Prose,* IV, 764–65; and Article 9 below, where the
Company sustains the charge that More sought a pastorate at Lyon and
elsewhere.

8. MS468, pp. 2–3. Milton refers to More's double-dealing in avoiding a trial *Complete Prose* IV, 758, 788–89, 800. The next four entries are nit-picking. Article 2 accuses More of having said that the Genevan pastors ignorantly preached "fateas et fables." Article 3 charges that he neglected his classes, teaching only three in April, 1648. Article 4 asked for the reason that he always took notes when in Company or Consistory meetings. Article 5 complains that he criticized members of the Company in public. More thrashes around in his answers, explaining that other duties interfered with his meeting classes and that he had the highest respect for the worthy members of the Company.

9. MS468, p. 3. Article 7 charges that he had declaimed against the Company "soubs la hasle de maison de ville" and had said that he would take his complaint into the streets. Article 8 alleges that he had written against the Company in various places.

10. MS468, p. 3. Milton says a good deal about Godofred Hotton (*Complete Prose,* IV, 708–709, 781, 813, 814, 815), who signed one of the testimonials offered in *Fides Publica.* Some of his information seems to have been derived from this article. The next seven charges indicate the extremes to which the Company went in attempting to saturate More's career with discredit. Article 10 claims that More scorned the authority of the Company; Article 11, that he eavesdropped on Company appearances before the Council; Article 12, that he consorted with a group of disguised persons; Article 13, that he came to church after the opening prayer and left before the closing prayer; Article 14, that among any complainants to the Company, two named De Tournes and La Pierre had filed assertions of his high-handedness; Article 15, that in preaching against his Low Country detractors he had blasphemed; Article 16, that he had not informed the Company of his correspondence with the Bishop of Armagh.

11. MS468, p. 7. Article 18 indicts More for lying; Article 19, for saying that it was a counsel of the devil that persuaded him to stay in Geneva; Article 20, for declaring that the Moderators of the Church amused themselves with trifles; Article 21, for uttering seditious political opinions; Article 23, for making several suspicious nocturnal visits to the house of a M. Rozet; Article 24, for preaching wildly about doctrine; Article 25, for proclaiming that the Consistory was an assembly of children and for confirming that opinion with an oath the following Thursday.

12. MS468, p. 7. Modern educators are not unfamiliar with comparable comstockery. About the only moral infirmity not alleged by the Company was homosexuality. But that came later in More's indictment by the Synod of Tergou (Stern, III, 299–303; *Complete Prose,* IV, 778). The next two items in the present list assert that in his oration on peace More taxed the doctors of the church with greed and ambition; and that in his

sermons he said the avaricious made God a banker, the gluttonous made
Him a cook, and the voluptuaries made Him a pimp.

13. MS468, p. 8. Milton's failure to make sport of this irrelevancy
suggests that he was not informed of it by Turretin, who seems to have
stuck to more serious questions. The late article in this review, number 31,
somewhat confusedly charged More with saying that he deliberately used
ambiguous language in order to give offense to those examining his
writings.

14. MS468, p. 10. Milton refers by name to these opponents; see
Complete Prose, IV, 798. The article preceding this one disputes More's
contention that he had communicated to the Company the articles signed
and sent to the Low Countries.

15. MS468, p. 11. Milton several times alludes to this heretical opinion; see *Complete Prose,* IV, 721, 790. Article 3 quotes More as declaring
he could not teach the doctrine he had been forced to endorse; Article 4
rebukes him for failing, after instruction, to give his students an orthodox
interpretation of grace.

16. MS468, p. 18. Eight intervening articles "touchant la doctrine"
deal with various theological subtleties on which More had likewise failed
to keep a promise of orthodoxy. Then come references to twenty-six
controversial passages in his oration on peace. Accusations of heresy
drawn from More's "dictats" occupy pages 18–23 of the manuscript; most
of them bear upon More's inclination to the "nouvelles doctrines" of
Saumur on predestination, grace and original sin.

17. MS468, p. 24. Despite the difference in given names, the second
item unquestionably refers to Claudia Pelletta, identified by Milton in the
Latin form of *Pelet* as More's mistress (*Complete Prose,* IV, 756–57). He
puns on Claudius—Claudia (p. 819–20) and on "plein Palais" (he calls
More *Palantinus adulter,* p. 739; "plein Palais" is still a well-known
section of Geneva). One *Pro Se Defensio* passage indicates how closely
Milton followed the MS468 account of More's escapade: "There is a
certain Claudia Pelletta, whom hereafter we shall call your mistress. . . .
Witness will not be lacking. First shall come forth that gardener who saw
you when you entered alone with the woman into that little garden
cottage; he saw when that Claudia of yours closed the doors; he saw you
afterwards come out openly embracing with the shameless woman. . . .
And others will come forth, whom those grave men who impeached you
have ready as witnesses (p. 756). . . . Soon among the mushrooms, and
the cabbage, and the kitchen vegetables, the mushroom being newly
tumescent, you did not indeed destroy Claudius, but you laid Claudia on
her back" (see p. 819 and note for explication of the involved bawdy pun-
ning). The note at pp. 777–78 reviews the evidence for Milton's knowledge of More's affairs with six or seven women during and after the
Genevan phase.

MILTON AS PHILOSOPHICAL POET

Robert West

Over the three hundred years since *Paradise Lost* was first published, its disparagers have charged it with many faults: blasphemy, Puritan hypocrisy, whiggery, British middle class stodginess, religious propagandizing, a deficiency of visual imagery, inconsistencies, arrogance, Satanism, dullness, deadness, and being the occasion of much dull, dead scholarship. It has, certainly, a special openness to another charge—that of being almost ideally suited to "Platonic" criticism, criticism concerned with values external to the work of art in works of art that themselves seem to claim such values. *Paradise Lost* is full of "thought" and "truths" that many a reader has valued for themselves.

We may suppose, of course, that whatever external values Milton sought to realize in *Paradise Lost,* he also understood very well that, as Maritain says, "Art operates for the good of the work done," not for some personal or social end. Milton met the requirements of the "good" of his work, its intrinsic requirements as narrative poetry, with a success to which, granted, not all Milton scholars have been attentive. In doing it he was, beyond any question, very much concerned also to win assent to "truths" of a most imposing scale. He intended to be a "philosophical

131

poet" in a way perhaps not basically different from the way that
Dostoyevski intended to be a philosophical novelist. Certainly
Milton's near-scholastic truths are very different from
Dostoyevski's near-existentialist ones. But each wanted the world
to understand what he tried to convey, and each found success
largely in shaping men's understanding.

For Milton to be a philosophical poet does not mean, of
course, that he was ahead of the philosophy of his time, as Proust
may have been of his, or was even abreast of it. Milton seems to
have had little sympathy with new ideas or ways of thought. Apparently he did not know or correspond with Descartes, Hobbes,
Boyle, Gassendi, or Henry More, and he refused to see Comen-
ius. His celebrated visit to Galileo, if it took place, did not much
influence his thought. He probably knew Mersenne as a biblical
commentator, but not as a mechanist philosopher. In fact, contemporary mechanism and empiricism, the inductive method,
and experimentation all seem unimportant in Milton's scheme of
thought. Milton was not interested in clearing away ancient pre-
conceptions, except, perhaps, some of Aristotle's, which he
looked on as crabbed. He was too authoritarian and too com-
mon-sense to relish the clean sweep that Bacon advocated and
Locke, Berkely and Hume were to pride themselves on. Milton
was simply not detached enough or flexible enough of mind for a
clear new philosophical vision. If, as Whitehead thought, philosophy is disclosure, fresh insight, the opening of windows, Milton
can hardly be called philosophical. He was rather a superbly
gifted confirmer of what his audience already believed and user
of ways of thinking already established. And he was an advocate,
not an investigator or discoverer. He inclined by nature to the
view that general truth had long been known and that by study
an able man might master it—and that he himself had in fact
mastered it. He had some adjustments to make to the picture of
things, and he made them with a firm hand. But he did not want
the established picture obscured, or for anyone to go really behind it.

None of these things suggest that Milton was a lackey of established philosophical interests, but simply that, like the great scholastics, he grounded his thinking in the Christian revelation.

One sense in which Milton was philosophical, though, was his life-long interest in the greatest questions of philosophy, including some that especially agitated his day: the nature and relation of matter and spirit, of freedom and responsibility, of man's origin and end. His thought on these things was not much like that of the more up-to-date of his contemporaries, and he did not originate important modern ways of thinking about them. But his thought was strong and in its great outlines, at least, clear. In *Paradise Lost* he gave it expression so influential that even his detractors have found it worth arguing against. He undoubtedly influenced thousands of English-speaking Christians in their grasp of the ideational content of biblical myth. Even now sophomores who have not yet read *Paradise Lost* nor been to Sunday school know with an inbred confidence that the serpent of Genesis was really Satan. No one can claim, of course, that they therefore "understand" the Christian solution of the problem of evil. This and similar vestiges, nevertheless, of Milton's account of original sin do remain firm in the mind of the west. A poet who treats the imposing matters that Milton did with some enduring effect is in a sense a philosophical poet.

In his own intention Milton would seem to have been a philosophical poet because he held that as poet he treated imposing matters with a kind of authority. He thought the poet an especially gifted teacher whose business it was to tell great truths in verse equal to the job, to convey important ideas soundly in the way special to poetry. He was a didactic, if you please, and a moralist in his practice and his theory. Especially he supposed that a mighty epic must show a beefier brand of "knowledge" than the delicate testimony to the "experimential reality" and the joy of sense and sensibility that a modern lyricist may value as supreme.

The knowledge that Milton set himself to transmit was some of

it naive, according to our views. His geography and his astronomy in *Paradise Lost,* though he took them from respected
sources, are not very impressive to modern geographers and
astronomers even if we allow poetic license. His physiology of
dreams and his angelology, on which he lavished pains, reflect a
kind of "science" totally dead now. Milton's reason for them
was that in *Paradise Lost* he was trying to deal with the largest
scale of the universe and had to offer the reader a world view. He
had to say how the whole of creation was arranged and how it
worked, and he showed his seriousness in offering what he
thought the best account of that his time afforded.

Still, we have to notice this about Milton's presentation of
astronomy and angelology and the rest of his "sciences": he
did not take any of it with the last seriousness. Unlike the scientists
who a few years ago showed their displeasure with Mr.
Velikovsky by badgering his publisher into giving up his book
Worlds in Collision, Milton did not suppose that "scientific"
knowledge is sacrosanct. He knew that his physiology and astronomy (and that of everybody else) was challengeable. The physical world of *Paradise Lost* he set up as a stage only. No doubt he
thought his stage well designed and constructed, but he did not
think its details important compared with the drama played on it.

The thing which Milton believed that he really knew about
and could transmit to his reader far more securely than he could
his astronomy was the cosmic drama of the Creator and his
creation. Man is God's creature, damaged by self-will, made
again by divine grace, and by his resort to it. The pageant of evil
and of man's involvement with it Milton found a stupendous
spectacle and an ennobling one in its grandeur and in its demonstration that basically God's providence brought good out of its
very opposite, so that even the Fall turned out a benefit. This
moral view of things was the kind of knowledge that Milton felt
belonged to the poet as a dedicated person, as a kind of priest
with a special means of making the truth known.

Skipping for a moment the question of whether Milton had

any better warrant to rely on his moral and religious knowledge than on his physical, let us touch the question of his confidence. How could he believe so securely that he knew?

If we compare Milton with another poet who wrote fewer than one hundred years after him and who also undertook to vindicate the ways of God to man, we can see how a poet's idea of his function changed after Milton. Pope's central critical principle he took from the French Neo-classicists: the poet's function is to please. Pope wrote, then, about God's ways with what amounts almost to flippancy, certainly with little of Milton's kind of seriousness. Pope lifted ideas from Bolingbroke—or from anyone that happened to appeal to him at the moment. He assumed little responsibility but for expression and for a decorousness that amounted to ideological conformity. Pope was, of course, a very different kind of man from Milton and writing for a very different audience. By Pope's time science was to the fore, with literature's enthusiastic approval. It had become clear, too, that science had but begun its career and clearer yet that it was a special way of knowing with so much already done and so much yet to do that the man of letters could not hope to master it without disciplines that would prevent his letters.

In Milton's formative days, on the other hand, the world, including the world of science, was still small. Medieval or Renaissance ideas of it were dominant. A great mind could master all, or suppose that it had. Robert Beal in the 1660's was able to say confidently that the friends of the great Robert Boyle might hope that in a few years he would "complete science." Henry More wrote with assurance of the afterworld as at hand just above men's heads. The physical universe itself seemed comparatively small, easily numbered. Thomas Heywood trying to show its immensity does the opposite when he says that an angel flying at 1000 miles an hour would span it from the utmost sphere to earth in six years. How petty a pace, distance and period compared with light years! In such a world as Milton's a poet could keep his confidence more easily than he could in Pope's world, much less ours. When Pope set out to vindicate God's ways, he probably had little in mind beyond elegantly re-stating some orthodox views in poetic language. But Milton really meant to justify God's actions to a world that could understand him. Milton was not propagandist nor advertiser nor yet entertainer. He was, in his own view, a seer and a truth-speaker.

How close, then, did Milton come to speaking truth? What special means did he have to know it? He conceived truth pretty much in scholastic terms: the conformity of the mind to reality as it is. Without supposing that he knew it wholly or absolutely, he undoubtedly felt in command of whatever of it a man could know in the ways he could know it. And I think that as far as moral truth goes—the truth that is sincerity, the responsible conformity of what is said to what is genuinely believed—Milton had as good means as most men before him or after. Though he may have had an imperious faith in his own learning, sensitiveness, and rationality that kept him from being an humbly self-critical man, still he did beyond any question labor prodigiously to perfect himself and he had great gifts. We probably ought to remember too that our equipment for knowing right conduct in ourselves is to say the least no better now than it was in Milton's time, which still profited from the prodigious thought given for centuries to personal morality. The discoveries in the natural sciences which have been the chief triumphs of the human mind since Milton have perhaps rather confused than clarified man's moral knowledge. By and large the findings of science have hurt our sense of personal responsibility for our opinions. One thing surely true of Milton was that he felt himself responsible and able to be.

Milton had some real means to know truth—if, indeed, any man has such means and we do not all deceive ourselves. He read the Bible (which of course he put first among his resources) and the thoughts of great thinkers before him. He had his own gifted mind and his intense self discipline, his determination to know. That's about all he had. But it is a great deal to seer at.

Milton understood very well that a poem is not a theorem nor a succession of them; but he did, nevertheless, make some major assertions in *Paradise Lost,* and he based them pretty firmly on his hard-bitten theological treatise *De Doctrina Christiana.* He evidently felt that poetry could give a more popular—and perhaps a "higher"—expression to religious views than the propositions of theology could, but that, whatever its expression, truth was basically one and of one kind. This is to say that Milton's ideas in *Paradise Lost* are not uncriticized ones, though they may be ideas of which no positivistic criticism has ever yet been possible. For a philosophical thinker to accept ideas that cannot be "proved" is entirely permissible. The thing that is outlawed for such a thinker is to believe what he refuses to criticize. Most of the ideas in *Paradise Lost* Milton had submitted in one way or another to prolonged criticism. That he did not reach Sartre's conclusions or Shaw's or many other conclusions that we now think up-to-date does not mean a real failure of his vocation as philosophical poet.

Consider, for instance, one of the central ideas in *Paradise Lost,* that of hierarchy—the idea that all creatures exist in a necessary order of rank according to their nearness to God on nature's scale. Rational creatures without impediment of body stand at the top of this scale, rational with bodies next, then sentient, and so on down. The scheme does not hold in the order of grace, which may put men above angels in some ways. Corollaries put man above woman, reason above passion, spirit above matter, learning above ignorance, virtue above wealth.

Obviously the idea of hierarchy is not in much favor today and has not been for a long time. In the year of Milton's death Spinoza wrote to a friend that it was beyond him to see how spirits more than other creatures could be said to express God, and that the excellence men traditionally attribute to some objects are not in the objects but in us as determined by our peculiar powers of apprehension. Spinoza's is the modern view. Certainly we do not hold men necessarily superior to women or their natural rulers.

And certainly we often value feeling above reason and disvalue such old favorites as thrift, chastity, and manners or valor, eloquence, and personal dignity.

On the other hand, the general idea of superior and inferior, of a sort of necessary rightness in the rule or the status or the compensation of some men or things over others is one that we can never get away from altogether. The fast horse is better to bet on than the slow one; the president ought to earn more than the governor and the well-trained engineer than the ill-trained. Certainly the president's responsibility is the larger, and we commit ourselves to the sound engineer's work more readily than to the unsound one's. Milton knew, of course that office does not always go with the ability to fill it, and the sound man is not always the predominating partner. But we can hardly deny that generally speaking he *ought* to be so. Somehow intelligence does seem superior to stupidity and virtue to wealth. No matter what the theory of relativity and its moral offshoots say, men naturally respond to the idea of hierarchy. It carries conviction however difficult the details are to sort out. To think so is not, of course, particularly philosophical in most of us. Our hierarchical ideas are very pragmatically shaped. But in Milton's time a reasoned idea of a particular natural hierarchy was still respectable, and it too was pragmatically defensible at many points. It took on dignity and worth in *Paradise Lost* with all sorts of rather convincing applications about discipline—largely self-discipline—and about freedom and equality. Milton understood that democracy among men is not a matter of strict equivalence, but of every sort serving in its place until by service it could rise.

The metaphysical basis for the order which Milton thought inherent in the world he found in God's creation of all things out of himself rather than out of nothing. This was a bold heresy that returned good practical dividends to Milton's system. Just how God managed creation according to *Paradise Lost* is open to dispute, but the poem does seem to say that somehow God withdrew his essence or divine nature from a part of Himself so as to leave it in a reduced condition which we many call raw or unorganized matter—or simply His material principle. Upon this, then, He put forth His power—the Word—and from it moulded the temporal universe, including the body and soul of man.

Granted that his statement raises more metaphysical and semantic questions than it answers, still it serves the philsophical imagination, and Milton makes a respectable fight for it in *De Doctrina Christiana.* We can defend him still at least on the ground that no account of universal origins can be really adequate.

What follows from Milton's insistence upon God's creation out of Himself is the unity and native goodness of created beings. Deriving from his view of creation Milton can insist upon the essential equality, the original uniform goodness, of every created essence. He can account then, for refinements that lift these essences by stages back toward God's own essence without denigrating the basic stuff at any stage. Finite spirit is superior to matter as being a stage toward God's own spirit; but it is at the same time continuous with matter, even in a sense identical with it. Milton has sometimes been called a materialist; he could just as well be called a spiritualist. He is sometimes called a pantheist, but one authority, at least, says he was rather a theopantist. God is all. The world is not his essence; but the world, visible and invisible, is rooted in His original propagation of matter from Himself.

Hardly any philosophers think in Milton's way now, of course; but a great many respected ones did think in it in Milton's day. Theirs was not the most productive thought for time to come; we call them philosophasters now—the Cambridge Platonists, for instance. But, they and Milton did cogitate with energy, persistence, and even power, on very great and basically important matters.

In his views of man and of man's mind and history, Milton rested on his views of ontology: as beings nearest to God (except angels) men had free will and so a worth beyond that of any mechanism, even the celestial, no matter how exact and immutable its movements. Man because of his origin and his high place in the hierarchy of being was responsible for his choices. He was in a finite way self-regulating, and so he was blameworthy for a failure in decision or for a faulty decision and praiseworthy for a due and sound one. Man's will and the rest of his mental powers functioned, nevertheless, largely through the agency of his body. Hence, though his will could not be coerced through his body, it might be moved indirectly by agency of some faculties that were controllable through body. By taking charge of the physiological bases of Eve's dreaming Satan could control her imagination and her understanding and so present false choices to her will. This notion Milton borrowed from demonology, not from Jungian psychology. Still he was talking of a kind of fragmentation of man's mental being. Milton probably had no clinical evidence for his belief, but he did have his intuition of his own discrete and assertive being. He had, too, all sorts of authority, though he parted with most of it in his view that man was not dichotomous, that the soul slept with the body after death.

As a thinker on history, Milton was (like most of us) pretty well confined by what authorities he had for the events of history. His dominating authority was, of course, scripture, and it clearly said to him that history began when God put forth His power on the substance from which He created the universe and that history would end with the total return to God of that part of His work that stood His test and with the isolation of the rest. This history as imparted by revelation was not allegorical in Milton's view. The myth he narrated in *Paradise Lost* he meant quite literally in its main elements. His view of history was a definite and confident one and from it followed the most literal justification of God's ways. How could it be, the question was, that in the creation of a benevolent Creator we find conditions that seem the work of malevolence? This is the problem of evil as Milton faced it. He undertook to justify what might seem malevolent in the human condition. Man, the facts show, made his own pains—or at least the occasion for God justly to inflict them. He made also the occasion for God mercifully to allow his recovery—an overriding good fortune that put man at last above even angels, since Christ did not die for them.

Plainly Milton did not submit his views on God's existence to such criticism as Jean-Paul Sartre has levelled at Christian belief in it and had no way to. Plainly, too, Milton was as interested as Sartre is in man's personal responsibily for his deeds and in the possibility that man may transcend his natural status. Milton considered the universe a just one originally made for man and recipient still of its Creator's will and attention which showed themselves most importantly in His grace to man. Such conviction kept him a long way from atheistical existentialism and from most of the rest of secular thought since his time. Milton was concerned in his poet's way with basic issues of philosophy. The poet's way is not the philosopher's way, but perhaps his engagement with the issues does entitle Milton to the adjective 'philosophical'.

University of Georgia

A NOTE ON MILTON'S DICTION

B. A. Wright

It may seem surprising that after centuries of assiduous editing a great number of archaic words and more especially uses of words in Milton's poems should remain either unglossed or glossed only incorrectly or inadequately. There are several reasons for this. In a living language some words and uses are continually becoming obsolete or archaic or passing away into dialect, or being replaced in normal speech and writing by other words. Some of these words are still familiar to readers acquainted with our past literature, though the reader's sense of the original distinctions in meaning and use will be more or less blurred and imprecise. In any case we have to take into account that these words and uses will be abandoned in time even by conservative poets and old-fashioned writers, and become quite obsolete. Secondly, there are some uses of words that are now quite obsolete but may be understood in a current use if this makes sense in the context. When one adds the fact that editors naturally copy from each other, the situation I call attention to no longer appears so surprising. The effects are serious in two main directions. First it can result in a misreading of the text. Secondly it can result in a loss of verbal sharpness, as of a worn coin, lending support to the notion of Milton's diction being flat, generalized and artificial, not based like Shakespeare's on the living language of the time; for this reason I mark with a dagger those uses common to the two poets; and no doubt some again will be surprised by the extent of this common ground between the English of Shakespeare and Milton.

The glossing of a text only some three to four centuries old requires then of an editor the unremitting scrutiny of a Bentley or Housman. Some editors of Milton are of course more alive to their duty than others, but all nod at more or less frequent intervals. A modern glossarist has the advantage of being able to rely on N.E.D. for a complete analysis of the history of the uses of English words and their differences in meaning and function; but even Homer nods, and I have tried to repay a little of my own immense debt to this great dictionary by noting its rare omissions and incorrect glosses in regard to Milton.

The following extracts are only of words beginning with *a,* omitting proper names, but they should suffice to give the general picture.

1. *Uses Not Noted or Incorrectly Glossed in N.E.D.*

antarctic   *adv.:* In the direction of the south pole of the earth; southwards. *obs.* P.L. IX. 79.

ask   *v. tr.: What was askt:* in reply to what was asked. P.L. IV. 899.

attendance   *sb.:* Attendant companions. *obs.* C. 314 (5).

aught   *sb.* (*pron.*): N.E.D. states that 'In Shakespeare, Milton, and Pope, *ought* and *aught* occur indiscriminately.' This is not true of Milton. The spelling in the early poems (Il P. 116, L. 120) is *ought* but in the later poems *aught;* it is true that at P.L. 1. 159 editions 1 and 2 give *ought* but the MS. reads *aught,* and the other *ought* at P.R. 1. 333 is obviously due to the printer.

2. *Not Noted in N.E.D. and Not Glossed or Incorrectly Glossed by Editors.*

anthem   *sb.:* A song of grief or mourning. *Obs.* N.O. 219.

arise   *v. intr:* To begin, come about. *arch.* P.L. II. 787.

3. Not Glossed by Editors

abate *v. tr.:* 1. To turn the edge, to blunt. *obs.#* P.R. II. 455. 2. *intr.* To decrease in size or bulk. *arch.#* P.L. XI. 841.

abide *v. tr.:* To endure, suffer, undergo. *obs.#* P. 20.

abode *sb.:* A temporary remaining; a stay. *obs.#* D.F. 1. 60.

absent *v. tr.:* To keep away, detain, withhold from being present. *obs.* P.L. IX. 372, X. 108.

accepted *ppl.a.:* Acceptable, approved, favoured. *obs.* P.L. XI. 46.

access *sb.:* 1. The action of coming to; coming into the presence; approach. *obs.* P.L. XII. 239. 2. Increase, addition, growth. *obs.* (replaced now by *accession*). P.L. IX. 310.

act *sb.:* 1. An activity, an active principle. *obs.* P.L. IX. 190. 2. *In act:* a) in the process, in the very doing. *obs.#* (Prince puts it under *b*) P.L. II. 109. b) in attitude or bearing (It. *in atto*). *obs.* P.L. IX. 668.

activity *sb.:* physical exercise, *spec.* gymnastics, athletics. *obs.* S.A. 1328.

address *sb.:* Duteous or courteous approach to a sovereign or lord. *obs.* D.L. 868.

adjoin *v.tr.:* To join on as an adjunct or supplement; to add. *arch.* P.R. I. 403.

admired of *pa.pple.:* of *obs.,* now by. S.A. 530.

advantage *sb.:* 1. A time of vantage, a favourable occasion, an opportunity. *obs.#* P.L. I. 327. IX. 258; P.R. II. 234. b) const. *on* (now *for*). *obs.* P.L. IX. 718. 2. Benefit, profit *of* (now *from*) *obs.#* S.A. 1259.

advantage *v.:* 1. *inpers.* To profit, benefit. *obs.* P.R. IV. 208. b) *absol. obs.* (unglossed exc. by Keightley's 'subjunctive mood'.) S.A. 255.

affront *sb.:* 1. An hostile encounter, an attack. *obs.* (glossed by Keightley as 'affronting' or 'facing', by Verity as 'meeting'). S.A. 531. 2. A meeting, encounter, *obs.* P.R. IV 444.

affront *v.tr.:* To confront one thing with another; to set face to face. *obs.#* (Richardson glosses 'meet face to face', Keightley 'face', Verity and Prince 'insult'.) P.L. I. 391.

after *adv,* and *prep, adv.:* Following an adj. *Famous after:* famous afterwards. *arch., rare.* P.R. II. 7. *prep.:* 1. In obedience to, in compliance or harmony with, according to a law. *obs.#* A. 72. 2. In a manner answering to, befitting, suiting. *arch.* P.L. VII. 311, 394, VIII. 343.

age *sb.: pl.* Future generations. *obs.* (glossed only by Richardson) P.L. XI. 326.

agitation *sb.:* The action of moving, stirring; motion. *obs.#* P.L. IX. 637.

aim *v.:* 1. *absol.* To guess, conjecture. *obs.#* P.L. XI. 884. 2. To devise, plan, aim at. *arch.#* P.R. IV. 208.

air *sb.:* Of a person: Attitude, gesture, manner, look. *arch.#* P.L. VIII. 476, IX. 459. b) Disposition, mood. *obs., rare.* (Keightley suggests a reference to the old medical notion of the arteries being filled with air.) P.L. XI. 542.

alarm *sb.:* A sudden attack, necessitating a rush to arms. *obs.#* P.L. X. 491.

allusion *sb.:* A symbolical likening: metaphor, parable, allegory. *obs.* P.L. X. 425.

also *adv.:* In the very manner of something else; in like manner, in the same, likewise, similarly, *obs.#* S. XX (*When I consider*). 14; P.L. III. 108, 823, V. 628, VIII. 220; P.R. I. 334.

amaze *sb.:* 1. Loss of presence of mind through terror; panic. *obs.* S. *XVI* (*Fairfax*).3; P.L. VI. 646; S.A. 1645. 2. Extreme astonishment, wonder. *arch* or *poet* # N.O. 69.

amazement *sb.:* 1. The condition of being mentally paralyzed, stupefaction. *obs.#* (glossed only by Prince, 1st cit.) P.L. I. 107; P.R. IV. 562. 2. Loss of presence of mind; bewilderment, perplexity (due to doubt as to what to do). *obs.#* P.R. I. 107. 3. Overwhelming fear or apprehension, consternation, alarm. *obs.#* C. 355 (6); P.L. II. 758, VI. 198.

amber *sb.:* An alloy of gold and silver. *obs.* P.L. VI. 759.

amber a.: Bright, shining (from *sb.* above). *obs.* (glossed only incorrectly.) L'A. 61; C. 332 (3).

amid *prep.:* Within the interior of a place. *obs.* P.L. IX. 401.

amuse *v.tr.:* A play on two senses: a) To cause to muse or stare; to bewilder, puzzle (*obs.*); b) To divert the attention (of an enemy) from one's real designs (*obs.*). Editors acknowledge 'The low puns' of Satan and Belial but do not stoop to explication. P.L. VI. 623.

ancient *a.:* 1. Of or belonging to time past; former, earlier, bygone. *arch.#* P.L. II. 394. 2. Of old renown; Long known to fame. Somewhat *arch.* V.Ex.98.

annoy *v.tr.: Mil.* To molest, assail, hurt, *arch.#* (unglossed exc. last cit.) P.L. VI. 369; P.R. III. 369; S.A. 578.

anon *adv.:* 1. Straightway. at once, instantly. *obs.#* P.L. I. 710. VI.

360, XI. 661. 2. Used loosely for: Soon. *Now literary.*# P.L. I. 325, 549, 759, VI. 564. XI. 433, 861, XII. 150; P.R. II. 285. 3. Now at this time, in contrast to *that time;* presently again, here again. *Now literary.*# L'A. 131; L. 169; P.R. I. 304.

answer   *v.tr.:* To correspond with, come up to. *?obs.* or *arch.* P.L. VII. 557; S.A. 1090.

antipathy   *sb.:* Contrariety of feeling, disposition, or nature; natural incompatibility; the oppos. of sympathy. *obs.*# P.L. X. 709.

apply   *v.tr.:* To address or direct (a spoken judgement) to. *obs.* P.L. X. 172.

appoint   *v.tr.:* To impute blame to, arraign. *obs., rare.* (Editors uncertain and at variance). S.A. 373.

apprehend   *v.tr:* To feel emotionally, be sensible of. *obs.*# P.L. V. 518.

approach   *v.intr.:* To draw near *to. arch.*# P.L. IV. 563.

approve   *v.tr.:* To pronounce to be good, commend. With *inf.* phrase as obj. *obs.*# P.L. IX. 1140.

arbitrement   *sb.:* arbitrament: The right or capacity to judge for oneself; freedom of will or choice. *obs.* P.L. VIII. 641.

arbor   *sb.:* A flower garden or bed. *obs.*# (The meaning might be the ordinary one of 'bower or shady retreat'.) P.L. IV. 626.

arboret   *sb.:* A little tree, a shrub. *arch.* or *obs.* P.L. IX. 437.

ardor   *sb.:* Zeal, fervour. Const. *to* (*obs.*) now *for.* P.L. VI. 66.

argue   *v. intr.:* To reason of (*obs.*) now *about.* P.L. II. 562.

arise   *v.intr.:* Now almost superseded by *rise* in ordinary language. 1. To get up from sitting or kneeling; to stand up. *arch.*# P.L. VIII. 644. b) With a play on sense 6. V. Ex. 91. 2. To get up from a fall. *obs.*# P.L. I. 330. 3. Of the sun, moon, stars; also *transf.,* of day, morning, evening. *arch.* and *poet*# P.L. V. 170, VII. 449, 582. 4. To spring forth (as a river from its source). *obs.* (With a play on sense 1.) V.Ex. 91.

arsenal   *sb.:* Dockyard (*obs.* exc. *Hist.*) of the Piraeus as the symbol of ancient Athenian naval power. (glossed incorrectly) P.R. IV. 270.

art   *sb.:* Skill in applying the principles of a special science; technical or professional skill. *obs.*# P.L. III. 602.

artificer   *sb.:* One who practices a skilled art; an artist. *obs.* P.R. IV. 59.

artist   *sb.:* 1. A scientist. *obs.* P.L. I. 288. 2. A skilled performer, an adept. *obs.* S.A. 1324.

ask   *v.tr.:* 1. to ask a person *of* (*arch*) i.e. *about* (something). P.L.

VII. 95. 2. To ask or request a thing *of* (*obs.*) i.e. *from* (a person). Ps II.16; P.L. II. 957, VIII. 53.

askanse   *adv.:* To eye askanse: to look at with envy, jealousy. *arch.#* (Now 'to look at with suspicion or mistrust') P.L. IV. 504.

aspect   *sb.:* The action of looking at anything; view, gaze. *obs.#* P.L. X. 454.

assailant   *a.:* Assailing, attacking, actively hostile. *obs.* S.A. 1693.

assassin-like   *adv.:* In the manner of a treacherous attacker. *obs.* P.L. XI. 293.

assay   *sb.:* (since the end of the 16th c. *essay* has replaced *assay* exc. for the testing of metals.) 1. The trial of something by tasting. *arch.#* P.L. XI. 747. 2. An attempt, endeavour. *arch.#* P.L. IV. 932. 3. Putting forth one's strength or energy, best effort. *arch.#* (glossed by Hughes but imprecisely.) P.L. VI. 153.

assay   *v.:* Now an archaic form of *essay,* exc. as applied to the testing of metals. 1. *tr.:* To put to the proof, to try (a person or thing); to test the nature, excellence or fitness of. *obs.#* P.R. II. 234. 2. To try with temptations or with things that influence; to tempt, to try to win over. *obs.#* (glossed by Verity and Hughes, but imprecisely.) P.L. III. 90. 3. To assail with words; to address. *obs.#* P.L. X. 865.

assign   *v.tr.:* To appoint authoritatively, prescribe (a course of action). *obs.* Const. with *in* (*obs.*) instead of *to.* P.L. V. 477.

astonisht   *ppl.a.:* 1. Stunned, stupified. *obs.#* P.L. I. 266. 2. Filled with consternation, dismayed, terrified. *obs.#* (glossed only by Prince, who puts it under 1.) P.L. II. 423.

astonishment   *sb.:* Stupor. *obs.* (glossed only by Keightley who says 'confusion, dismay'.) P.L. I. 317.

at   *prep.:* 1. *At interview:* in mutual view. *obs. rare.* P.L. VI. 555. 2. *At choice:* at pleasure. *obs.#* P.L. V. 499.

attain   *v.tr.:* 1. To get to know; find out. *obs.* P.L. VII. 115, VIII. 70, 412. 2. *intr.* To succeed in reaching a state or condition. With *inf.* of purpose. *obs.* P.L. IX. 726.

attempt   *v.tr.:* 1. To try with temptations, to try to win over, seduce, entice; to tempt. *obs.#* P.L. IX. 369, 1180, X. 8, P.R. II. 205. 2. To make an attack on the chastity of, to try to ravish or seduce. *obs.#* C. 405 (6). 3. *absol.* To attack, assail, assault. *arch.* (glossed by Prince only.) P.L. II. 357.

attempt   *sb.:* 1. A warlike enterprise; an attack. *obs.#* P.L. I. 642, VII. 609. 2. Temptation, seduction. *obs.#* P.L. IX. 295, 481, 1149; P.R. IV. 180.

attempter   *sb.:* One who makes a criminal attempt (against a rightfully established authority); an assaillant. *obs.* P.R. IV. 603.

attend   *v. intr.:* 1. To turn one's ear to; to listen, heed. *arch.#* P.L. VIII. 247, XII. 12.2. With *inf.* To apply oneself, endeavour, *obs.* S. IX *(Lady).*9.

attendance   *sb.:* A body of attendants, train of servants, retinue, *obs.* (Inadequately glossed.) P.L. X. 80.

attribute   *v.intr.:* 1. To bestow, concede, assign *to* anyone, as his right. *obs.* P.L. VIII. 12. 2. *Attribute much* or *less:* to ascribe great (or less than enough) importance *to,* to hold in high (or low) estimation. *obs.* P.L. VIII. 565, IX. 320.

author   *sb.:* 1. The person to whom anything owes its origin or existence; the inventor, constructer, or founder. *obs.* now in respect of anything material. P.L. X. 356. b) One who instigates or authorises; the prompter or mover. *obs.#* P.L. III. 122.

avenger   *sb.:* He who takes revenge or punishes (an offender). *obs.* P.L. X. 241.

await   *v.tr.:* To watch, lie in wait for, waylay, *obs.* S.A. 1197.

aware   *a.:* Watchful, vigilant, on their guard. *obs.* P.L. VI. 547.

awe   *sb.:* Power to inspire fear or reverence; overawing influence. *arch.#* C. 32; P.L. VIII. 558.

axle   *sb.:* The imaginary line about which a planet, including the earth, revolves. *obs. exc. poet.* P.L. II. 926, VIII. 165.

axletree   *sb.: fig.* The spindle or axle of the chariot of the sun. *obs.* N.O. 84.

University of Southampton

TH'UPRIGHT HEART
AND PURE

Thirty years ago, F. R. Leavis—the intellectual leader of a minority group of Cambridge critics, whose methodical and uncompromising destruotion of reputations periodically enlivened the pages of critical literature of the time—solemnly pronounced that *Paradise Lost* is "dull and empty." Ezra Pound, who reigned over a kindred critical circle on this side of the Atlantic, complained of Milton's "gross and utter stupidity." Ironically, however, some of the keenest critical interpretation and revaluation of Milton's works was in the making, not only inspired by Milton's works but also provoked by these early attacks. Stalwart defenders, hastening to the rescue of the poet, engaged themselves with Milton's ideology and poetic sensibility, as well as with textual appreciation and exegesis.

Today, these times of theological ferment, Milton's religious epics assumed a new relevance. And, thankfully, the poet's works are receiving, and will continue to receive, masterful treatment by the literary world's most estimable scholars. In this volume, Amadeus P. Fiore, O.F.M., to commemorate the tercentenary of the publication of *Paradise Lost*, has assembled eleven essays by the most outstanding and authoritative Miltonists living today: Merritt Y. Hughes investigates and defends Milton's "Paradise of Fools" in the light of its possible Italian sources, while Wayne Shumaker investigates the epic itself against the rich background of Italian epic literature. Maurice Kelley contributes further to his work on Milton's theology by examining the first phase of *De Doctrina Christiana;* and William B. Hunter, Jr. studies Milton's Satan in the light of the dynamic Monarchian persuasion. Edward Le Comte discusses a facet of